Eye-Catching Quilts

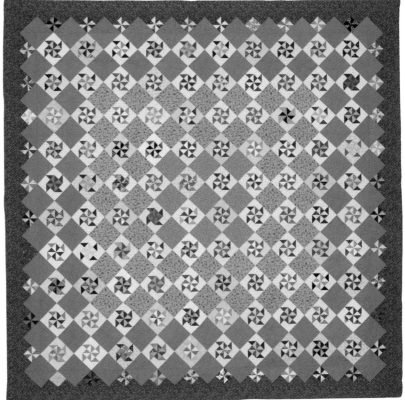

16 Designs from the Experts at
Quiltmaker
MAGAZINE

Martingale
Create with Confidence

Eye-Catching Quilts: 16 Designs from the Experts at *Quiltmaker* Magazine

© 2012 by *Quiltmaker* Magazine

Martingale®
19021 120th Ave. NE, Ste. 102
Bothell, WA 98011-9511 USA
ShopMartingale.com

Quiltmaker, ISSN 1047-1634, is published bimonthly by Creative Crafts Group, LLC, 741 Corporate Circle, Suite A, Golden, CO 80401, www.quiltmaker.com.

Printed in China
17 16 15 14 13 12   8 7 6 5 4 3 2 1

Library of Congress Cataloging-in-Publication Data is available upon request.

ISBN: 978-1-60468-239-7

Mission Statement
Dedicated to providing quality products and service to inspire creativity.

Credits:

President & CEO: Tom Wierzbicki

Editor in Chief: Mary V. Green

Design Director: Paula Schlosser

Managing Editor: Karen Costello Soltys

Technical Editor: Nancy Mahoney

Copy Editor: Marcy Heffernan

Production Manager: Regina Girard

Cover & Text Designer: Connor Chin

Photographer: Mellisa Karlin Mahoney (except as noted)

Photo of "Duette" on pages 6 and 10, "Periwinked" on page 43, and "Piece and Goodwill" on page 85 by Tim Benko of Benko Photographics.

Photo of "Raspberry Truffles" on page 32 and "Pinwheel Party" on page 56 by Joe Hancock Studio.

Contents

Introduction

Surrounded by creativity and inspiration, I have a really fun job. And it's not just the quilts, the fabrics, and the colors here in the office; I'm also surrounded by an amazing staff. *Quiltmaker* magazine began in 1982 with people who were not only passionate about quilting but who were also talented designers. And that legacy continues today. We all enjoy fabric and love to quilt, but we have different tastes and styles—and that helps us create a wide range of patterns that appeal to many quiltmakers.

This book is filled with fun and original quilts designed by *Quiltmaker* staff, both current and former. You'll find a wide range of techniques and skill levels among our quilts— from quick and easy designs to masterpieces that will be heirlooms for generations to come. I think as you look through these designs, you'll be able to discover something about each of our personalities and what inspires us.

You'll also find that almost every pattern here has a color option to inspire your quiltmaking in new directions. That's one of the fun parts of working at *Quiltmaker*—taking a pattern and looking for new ways to interpret it. Sometimes it's just a new color palette, but sometimes value changes can make the pattern look like a brand new design. And we never leave you wondering how to quilt your top—every *Quiltmaker* pattern also has a quilting plan to give you ideas for finishing your quilts, with original quilting motifs in many cases.

I hope you enjoy the quilts you make from this book—as much as we've enjoyed bringing them to you!

June Dudley
Quiltmaker, Editor in Chief

Carolyn used a couple of her favorite design elements—a two-block combination and miniature patches—in this pair of quilts. After you make the twin-size quilt, whip up the coordinating miniature quilt. It's perfect for a little girl and her doll, or just to accessorize a room.

Designed and sewn by Carolyn Beam, *Quiltmaker* creative editor; quilted by Kim Waite.

Finished Twin-Size Quilt: 73" x 88"
Finished Blocks: 9" x 9"
Finished Doll-Sized Quilt: 21¼" x 21¼"
Finished Blocks: 4½" x 4½"

Materials

Yardage is based on 42"-wide fabric. Materials are sufficient to make both quilts.

2¾ yards of red print for blocks, sashing, and outer border

2⅝ yards of cream tone-on-tone print for blocks and inner border

2¼ yards of taupe print #1 for blocks and setting triangles

1⅓ yards of taupe-striped print for middle border and binding

1 yard of faded-red print for sashing

⅞ yard of taupe print #2 for blocks and sashing

⅝ yard of faded-red tone-on-tone print for blocks

7¼ yards of backing fabric for twin quilt

¾ yard of backing fabric for doll quilt

81" x 96" piece of batting for twin quilt

25" x 25" piece of batting for doll quilt

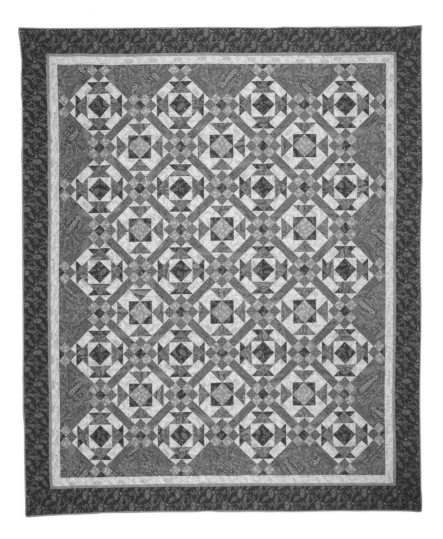

Cutting for Twin-Size Quilt

From the *lengthwise grain* of the red print, cut:
  2 outer-border strips, 5" x 81"
  2 outer-border strips, 5" x 75"
  80 squares, 2⅜" x 2⅜" (A)
  20 squares, 3½" x 3½" (B)
  31 squares, 2" x 2" (F)
  12 squares, 4¼" x 4¼" (G)
  9 squares, 2⅜" x 2⅜"; cut in half diagonally to
    yield 18 triangles (H)

From the cream tone-on-tone print, cut:
  8 inner-border strips, 2" x 42"
  128 squares, 2⅜" x 2⅜" (A)
  40 squares, 3" x 3"; cut in half diagonally to yield
    80 triangles (C)
  128 rectangles, 2" x 3½" (E)
  48 squares, 2⅜" x 2⅜"; cut in half diagonally to
    yield 96 triangles (H)

From the taupe print #1, cut:
  64 squares, 3⅞" x 3⅞"; cut in half diagonally to
    yield 128 triangles (D)

  4 squares, 14" x 14"; cut into quarters diagonally
    to yield 16 triangles (J) (2 triangles are extra)
  2 squares, 7¼" x 7¼"; cut in half diagonally to
    yield 4 triangles (K)

From the faded-red tone-on-tone print, cut:
  128 squares, 2" x 2" (F)

From the taupe print #2, cut:
  12 squares, 3½" x 3½" (B)
  160 squares, 2" x 2" (F)

From the faded-red print, cut:
  80 rectangles, 2" x 6½" (I)

From the taupe-striped print, cut:
  8 middle-border strips, 1" x 42"
  2¼"-wide bias-binding strips to total 330"*

** If you are making both quilts, cut the middle-border
strips for both quilts from the taupe-striped print
before cutting the strips for the bias binding.*

Making the Twin-Size Blocks and Sashing Units

Press the seam allowances in the direction indicated.

1. Referring to "Triangle Squares" on page 90, use the red and cream A squares to make 160 triangle-square units.

Make 160.

2. Sew four cream C triangles to each red B square to make a center unit. Make 20 units.

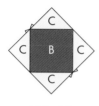

Make 20.

3. Lay out one center unit, four taupe-print #1 D triangles, four cream E rectangles, eight triangle-square units, and four faded-red F squares as shown. Sew the pieces together into rows and press. Sew the rows together to complete block W; press. Repeat to make a total of 20 blocks.

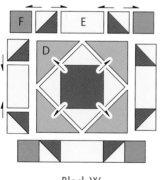

Block W.
Make 20.

4. Refer to "Fast Flying Geese" on page 9 and use the cream A squares and the red G squares to make 48 flying-geese units.

Make 48.

5. Sew cream H triangles to adjacent sides of a faded-red F square. Then add a taupe-print #1 D triangle to make a corner unit. Make 48 of these units.

Make 48.

6. Lay out four corner units, four flying-geese units, four cream E rectangles, and one taupe-print #2 B square. Sew the E rectangles to the flying-geese units and press. Then join the pieces into rows and press. Sew the rows together to complete block X; press. Repeat to make a total of 12 blocks.

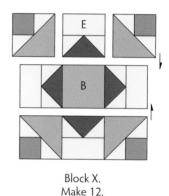

Block X.
Make 12.

7. Join taupe-print #2 F squares to both ends of a faded-red-print I rectangle to make a sashing unit. Make 80 units.

Make 80.

Assembling the Twin-Size Quilt

1. Join the blocks, sashing units, and taupe-print #1 J triangles as shown in the quilt assembly diagram to make diagonal rows. Press the seam allowances toward the sashing units.

2. Join the sashing units, red F squares, and red H triangles as shown to make sashing rows. Press the seam allowances toward the sashing units.

3. Sew the rows together and add a taupe-print #1 K triangle to each corner. Press the seam allowances toward the sashing units.

Twin-size quilt assembly

4. Sew the cream inner-border strips together end to end to make a long strip. Referring to "Squared Borders" on page 93, measure, cut, and sew the strips to the sides, top, and bottom of the quilt top.

5. Sew the taupe-striped middle-border strips together end to end to make a long strip. Measure, cut, and sew the strips to the sides, top, and bottom of the quilt top.

6. Measure, cut, and sew the 81"-long red outer-border strips to the sides of the quilt top. Then add the 75"-long red outer-border strips to the top and bottom of the quilt top.

Quilting and Finishing

Refer to "Basic Quiltmaking Lessons" on page 89 for more information on quilting and finishing your quilt.

1. Mark the Moonflower quilting pattern on page 13 horizontally over the quilt surface as shown in the quilting placement diagram, staggering the motifs in every other row. Notice that the motif shown in red has scallops surrounding the entire flower. Mark partial motifs at the ends of rows as needed.

Fast Flying Geese

This technique offers a shortcut for making multiple matching flying-geese units.

1. Align two cream A squares on opposite corners of a red G square, right sides together. Draw a diagonal line as shown and then stitch ¼" from both sides of the line. Cut the squares apart on the marked line. Press the seam allowances toward the resulting cream triangles.

2. Place a cream A square on the remaining red corner of each unit from step 1. Draw a line from corner to corner as shown and sew ¼" from both sides of the line. Cut on the marked lines and press the seam allowances toward the cream triangles. Each set of one G square and four A squares will make four flying-geese units.

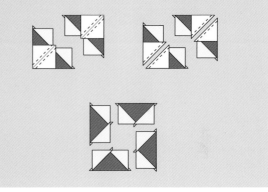

2. Layer and baste together the backing, batting, and quilt top.

3. Quilt the marked motifs.

4. Bind the quilt using the taupe-striped strips.

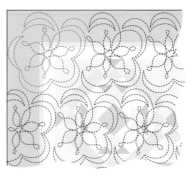

Quilting placement

Dolly Duette

Cutting for Doll Quilt

From the red print, cut:
2 outer-border strips, 2½" x 20"
2 outer-border strips, 2½" x 24"
16 squares, 1⅝" x 1⅝" (L)
4 squares, 2" x 2" (M)
4 squares, 1¼" x 1¼" (Q)
1 square, 2¾" x 2¾" (R)
4 squares, 1⅝" x 1⅝"; cut in half diagonally to
   yield 8 triangles (S)

From the cream tone-on-tone print, cut:
2 inner-border strips, 1¼" x 18"
2 inner-border strips, 1¼" x 19"
20 squares, 1⅝" x 1⅝" (L)
4 squares, 2¾" x 2¾"; cut into quarters diagonally
   to yield 16 triangles (N)
20 rectangles, 1¼" x 2" (P)
4 squares, 1⅝" x 1⅝"; cut in half diagonally to
   yield 8 triangles (S)

From the taupe print #1, cut:
10 squares, 2⅜" x 2⅜"; cut in half diagonally to
   yield 20 triangles (O)
1 square, 7⅝" x 7⅝"; cut into quarters diagonally
   to yield 4 triangles (U)
2 squares, 4⅛" x 4⅛"; cut in half diagonally to
   yield 4 triangles (V)

From the faded-red tone-on-tone print, cut:
20 squares, 1¼" x 1¼" (Q)

From the taupe print #2, cut:
1 square, 2" x 2" (M)
32 squares, 1¼" x 1¼" (Q)

From the faded-red print, cut:
16 rectangles, 1¼" x 3½" (T)

From the taupe-striped print, cut:
2 middle-border strips, ¾" x 19"
2 middle-border strips, ¾" x 20"
2¼"-wide bias-binding strips to total 94"*

** If you are making both quilts, cut the middle-border
strips for both quilts from the taupe-striped print
before cutting the strips for the bias binding.*

Making the Doll-Quilt Blocks and Sashing Units

1. Refer to "Triangle Squares" on page 90 and use
the red and cream L squares to make 32 triangle-
square units.

Make 32.

2. Sew four cream N triangles to each red M square
to make a center unit. Press the seam allowances
toward the cream triangles.

3. Lay out one center unit, four taupe-print #1 O
triangles, four cream P rectangles, eight triangle-
square units, and four faded-red Q squares as
shown. Sew the pieces together into rows. Press the
seam allowances in the direction indicated. Sew the

rows together to complete block Y; press. Repeat to make a total of four blocks.

Block Y.
Make 4.

4. Refer to "Fast Flying Geese" on page 9 and use the cream L squares and the red R square to make four flying-geese units.

Make 4.

5. Sew cream S triangles to adjacent sides of a faded-red Q square. Press the seam allowances toward the triangles. Then sew a taupe-print #1 O triangle to the triangle unit to make a corner unit. Press the seam allowances toward the O triangle. Make four of these units.

6. Lay out the corner units, the flying-geese units, four cream P rectangles, and the taupe-print #2 M square. Sew the P rectangles to the flying-geese units. Then join the pieces into rows and press. Sew the rows together to complete block Z; press.

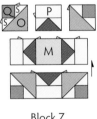

Block Z.
Make 1.

7. Join taupe-print #2 Q squares to both ends of a faded-red T rectangle to make a sashing unit. Make 16 units.

Make 16.

Assembling the Doll Quilt

1. Join the blocks, sashing units, and taupe-print #1 U triangles as shown in the quilt assembly diagram to make diagonal rows. Press the seam allowances toward the sashing units.

2. Join the sashing units, red Q squares, and red S triangles as shown to make sashing rows. Press the seam allowances toward the sashing units.

3. Sew the rows together and add a taupe-print #1 V triangle to each corner. Press the seam allowances toward the sashing units.

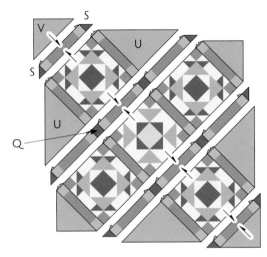

Doll-quilt assembly

4. Measure, cut, and sew the 18"-long cream inner-border strips to the sides of the quilt top. Then add the 19"-long cream inner-border strips to the top and bottom of the quilt top.

5. Measure, cut, and sew the 19"-long taupe-striped middle-border strips to the sides of the quilt top. Then add the 20"-long taupe-striped middle-border strips to the top and bottom of the quilt top.

6. Measure, cut, and sew the 20"-long red outer-border strips to the sides of the quilt top. Then add the 24"-long red outer-border strips to the top and bottom of the quilt top.

Quilting and Finishing

Refer to "Basic Quiltmaking Lessons" on page 89 for more information on quilting and finishing your quilt.

1. Layer and baste together the backing, batting, and quilt top.

2. The Moonflower or Mini Moonflower quilting patterns (below and opposite) can be quilted in continuous horizontal rows without marking as shown in the quilting placement diagram.

Quilting placement

3. Bind the quilt using the taupe-striped bias-binding strips.

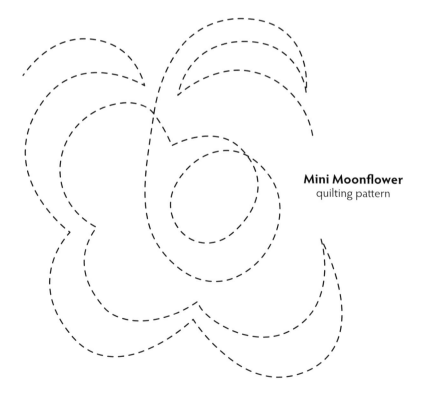

Mini Moonflower
quilting pattern

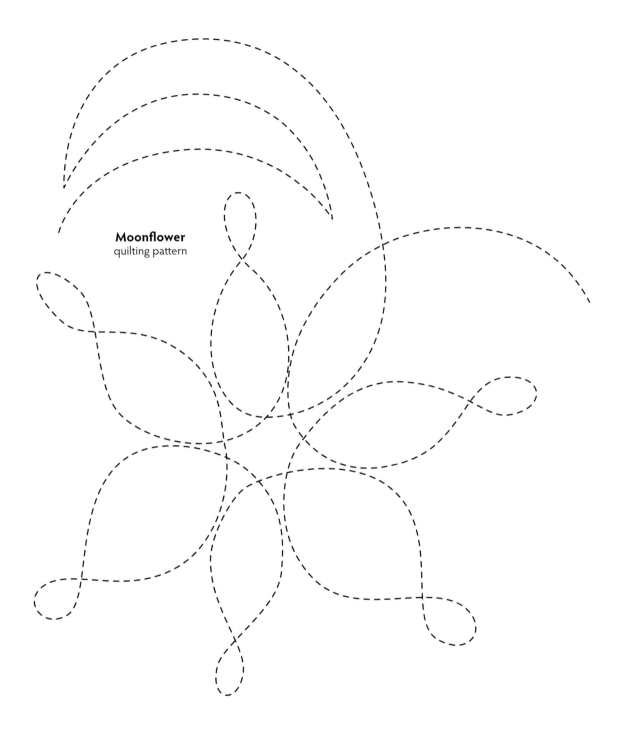

Moonflower
quilting pattern

East meets West in this quilt with a strip setting. The large patches are a great place to showcase large-scale prints or quilting motifs. Make the coordinating pillowcases for a calming bedroom ensemble.

Designed by Theresa Eisinger, former *Quiltmaker* graphic designer; made by Kim Waite.

Finished Quilt: 89" x 99½"

Materials

Yardage is based on 42"-wide fabric. Materials are for quilt only; for each pillowcase, you'll need an additional ¾ yard of the light-gray print, ⅓ yard of the dark-green print, and ⅙ yard of the brown print. For complete instructions for making the pillowcase, visit quiltmaker.com.

6 yards of dark-green print for background, sashing, and binding

2 yards of light-gray print for blocks

1⅛ yards of medium-taupe print for blocks

1 yard of brown print for blocks

8⅝ yards of backing fabric

97" x 108" piece of batting

Cutting

From the brown print, cut:
    104 squares, 3" x 3" (A)
    6 squares, 5½" x 5½" (E)

From the *lengthwise grain* of the dark-green print, cut:
    8 sashing strips, 4½" x 99½"
    18 squares, 8⅜" x 8⅜"; cut into quarters diagonally to yield 72 triangles (F)
    6 squares, 8" x 8"; cut in half diagonally to yield 12 triangles (H)

From the remaining dark-green print, cut:
    11 binding strips, 2¼" x 42"
    50 squares, 4¾" x 4¾"; cut into quarters diagonally to yield 200 triangles (B)
    8 squares, 2⅝" x 2⅝"; cut in half diagonally to yield 16 triangles (C)
    8 squares, 4" x 4" (D)

From the medium-taupe print, cut:
    42 squares, 5½" x 5½" (E)

From the light-gray print, cut:
    18 squares, 10½" x 10½" (G)

Making the Quilt Top

1. For row 1, join dark-green B triangles to opposite sides of a brown A square to make 26 units as shown. Press the seam allowances toward the A squares. Join the units and press the seam allowances to one side. Sew dark-green C triangles to both ends; press. Sew dark-green D squares to both ends to complete the row. Press the seam allowances toward the D squares. Add a dark-green sashing strip to each side of the row. Repeat to make four of row 1.

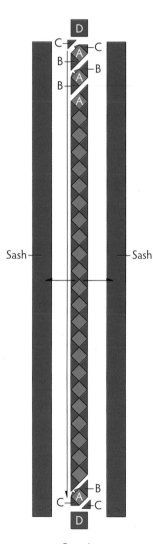

Row 1.
Make 4.

2. For row 2, join a brown E square, a medium-taupe E square, and a dark-green F triangle as shown at right. Press the seam allowances in the direction indicated. Make two of these units.

3. Join a dark-green F triangle to a medium-taupe E square. Press the seam allowances toward the E square. Make two units.

4. Sew dark-green F triangles to adjacent sides of medium-taupe E squares to make 10 triangle units. Press the seam allowances toward the F triangles.

5. Sew the units from steps 2–4 and six light-gray G squares together as shown. Press the seam allowances toward the G squares. Join dark-green H triangles to both ends to complete row 2. Press the seam allowances toward the H triangles. Make three of row 2.

Row 2.
Make 3.

6. Matching centers and ends, sew the rows together as shown in the quilt assembly diagram.

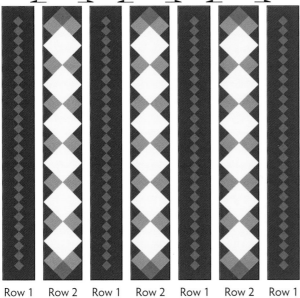

Row 1 Row 2 Row 1 Row 2 Row 1 Row 2 Row 1

Quilt assembly

Quilting and Finishing

Refer to the quilting placement diagram and use the quilting patterns on page 18. Refer to "Basic Quilt-making Lessons" on page 89 for more information on quilting and finishing your quilt.

1. Mark the Ginkgo Leaf quilting pattern three times in the light-gray G squares as shown, rotating the motif 120° after each marking and matching the center mark each time.

2. Mark the Ginkgo Leaf quilting pattern at the ends of each row 2 as shown, reversing the motif as shown in red.

3. Mark the Curly Vine quilting pattern in the remaining E squares as shown.

4. Use the Gentle Wave quilting pattern for marking the curved lines in the dark-green background as shown.

5. Layer and baste together the backing, batting, and quilt top.

6. Quilt the E squares and G squares in the ditch as shown. Quilt the marked lines.

7. Bind the quilt using the dark-green strips.

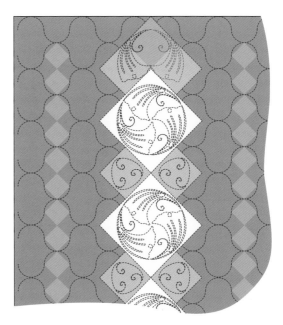

Quilting placement

Color Option

Sweet Serenity

Let a calming array of teals and purples soothe your soul. A luscious teal ikat adds appealing texture to this design.

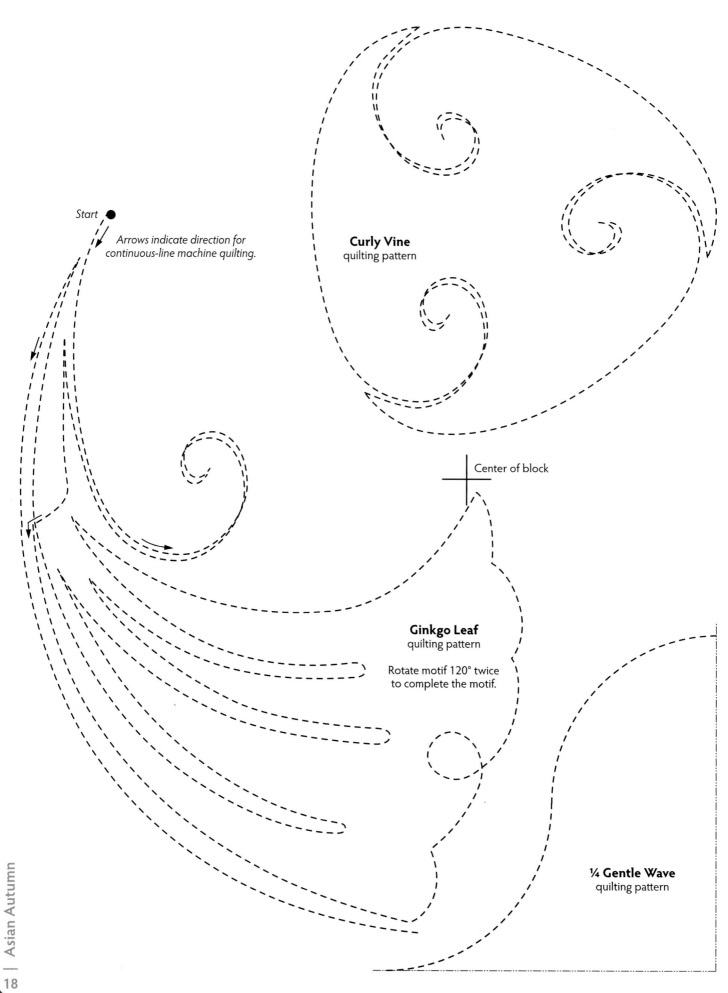

Start

Arrows indicate direction for
continuous-line machine quilting.

Curly Vine
quilting pattern

Center of block

Ginkgo Leaf
quilting pattern

Rotate motif 120° twice
to complete the motif.

¼ Gentle Wave
quilting pattern

Today's luscious fabrics turn out leaves almost as beautiful as Mother Nature's. Notice the yellow aspen leaf is shaded, with a dark and a light side; the red maple leaf gradates from light at the tip to dark at the stem. While Erin Wilcoxon loves fall colors, her inspiration came from leaf-block designs by Bea Yurkerwich and Mary Austin.

Designed by Erin Wilcoxon, former *Quiltmaker* art director; made by Mickie Swall.

Finished Quilt: 55" x 70"
Finished Blocks: 7½" x 7½"

Materials

Yardage is based on 42"-wide fabric unless otherwise noted. Although fabric amounts for foundation piecing are adequate, you may need more if you cut very generous pieces.

3¼ yards of cream print for blocks

2 yards of multicolored print for outer border and binding

1 yard *total* of assorted brown, orange, and red prints for stems and block Z

¾ yard *total* of assorted green prints for block X

¾ yard *total* of assorted green, yellow, and gold prints for block Y

½ yard of orange print for inner border

3⅝ yards of backing fabric

59" x 74" piece of batting

Cutting

Patterns for pieces B, J, K, K reversed, and M are on page 23. For detailed instructions, refer to "Making Plastic Templates" on page 90 as needed.

From the cream print, cut:
26 squares, 3" x 3" (A)
26 squares, 3⅜" x 3⅜"; cut in half diagonally to yield 52 triangles (C)
8 rectangles, 1½" x 7" (D)
9 rectangles, 1½" x 8" (E)
33 squares, 2⅜" x 2⅜"; cut in half diagonally to yield 66 triangles (H)
22 rectangles, 2" x 3½" (I)
11 K pieces
11 reversed K pieces
11 squares, 3½" x 3½" (L)
12 rectangles, 4¼" x 8" (N)
1 rectangle, 7" x 8" (O)
1 rectangle, 8" x 15½" (P)
5 squares, 8" x 8" (Q)
2 rectangles, 4¼" x 15½" (R)

From the assorted brown, orange, and red prints, cut:
13 B stems
11 squares, 2" x 2" (F)
66 rectangles, 2" x 3⅞"; refer to the diagram below to cut 33 G and 33 G reversed pieces
11 J pieces
11 M stems

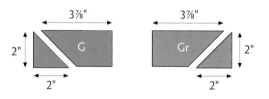

From the assorted green prints, cut:
39 squares, 3" x 3" (A)
26 squares, 3⅜" x 3⅜"; cut in half diagonally to yield 52 triangles (C)

From the orange print, cut:
7 inner-border strips, 2" x 42"

From the *lengthwise grain* of the multicolored print, cut:
   2 outer-border strips, 4" x 66"
   2 outer-border strips, 4" x 58"
   5 binding strips, 2¼" x 55"

Making the Blocks

1. To make block X, prepare the three edges of each B stem that will not be caught in a seam for "Turned-Edge Appliqué" as described on page 92. Place a prepared stem on a cream A square as shown in the diagram following step 2 and blind-stitch in place.

Blind stitch

2. Join the cream and green C triangles to make triangle-square units. Lay out an appliquéd A square, three green A squares, four triangle-square units, and one cream A square in three rows as shown. Join the pieces in each row and press the seam allowances as indicated. Sew the rows together and press to complete the block. Repeat to make 13 of block X.

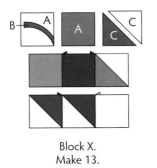

Block X.
Make 13.

3. Make eight copies each of the foundation patterns on pages 23 and 24. Paper piece the units in numerical order. Press and trim after adding each piece. Refer to "Foundation-Piecing Basics" on page 91 for detailed instructions as needed.

4. Join the units and press the seam allowances to one side. Add the cream D and E rectangles to complete the block. Repeat to make eight of block Y.

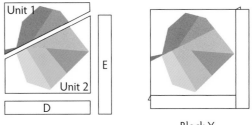

Block Y.
Make 8.

5. To make block Z, prepare the three edges of each M stem that will not be caught in a seam for turned-edge appliqué. Place a prepared stem on a cream L square as shown in the diagram following step 7 and blindstitch in place.

6. Sew cream H triangles to G and G reversed pieces as shown below. Join K and K reversed pieces to each J piece. Press the seam allowances in the direction indicated.

7. Lay out the appliquéd L squares, the pieces from step 6, and one assorted F square in three rows as shown. Join the pieces in each row and press. Sew the rows together and press to complete the block. Repeat to make 11 of block Z.

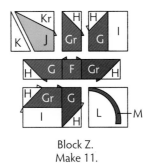

Block Z.
Make 11.

Assembling the Quilt Top

1. Join the blocks, the last E rectangle, and the cream N, O, P, Q, and R pieces into sections, making sure to orient the blocks as shown in the quilt assembly diagram. Sew the sections together to complete the quilt center. Press the seam allowances in the direction indicated.

2. Remove the foundation papers from the Y blocks.

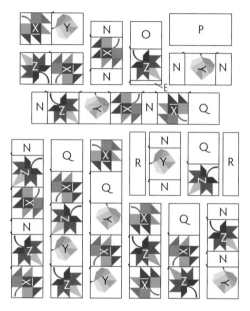

Quilt assembly

3. Join the orange inner-border strips end to end to make a long strip. Referring to "Squared Borders" on page 93, measure, cut, and sew the strips to the sides, top, and bottom of the quilt center.

4. Measure, cut, and sew the 66"-long multicolored outer-border strips to the sides of the quilt top. Then add the 58"-long multicolored outer-border strips to the top and bottom of the quilt top.

Quilting and Finishing

Refer to "Basic Quiltmaking Lessons" on page 89 for more information on quilting and finishing your quilt.

1. Layer and baste together the backing, batting, and quilt top.

2. Quilt the leaves in the ditch; then echo quilt inside the shapes as shown in the quilting placement diagram. Quilt random wavy lines across the quilt, interrupting the stitching at the leaves. Quilt the inner border in the ditch. Quilt a wavy line through the center of the outer border.

3. Bind the quilt using the 2¼" multicolored strips.

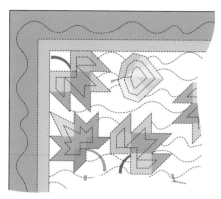

Quilting placement

Color Option

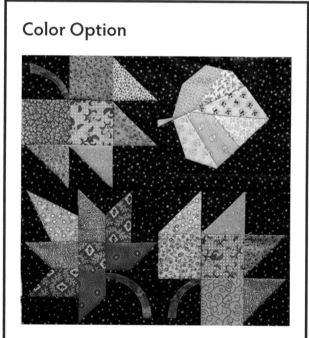

Autumn Nights

Subtle prints create a subdued, old-fashioned look in this dark-background variation. These colors create a warm and cozy atmosphere on a chilly autumn night.

Foundation patterns are the reverse of the finished block.

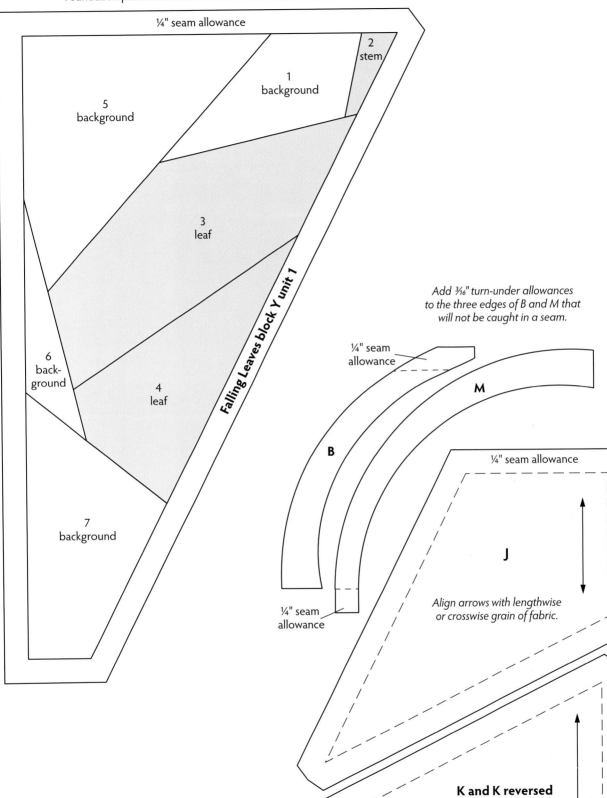

¼" seam allowance

1
background

2
stem

5
background

3
leaf

Falling Leaves block Y unit 1

6
back-
ground

4
leaf

7
background

*Add ³⁄₁₆" turn-under allowances
to the three edges of B and M that
will not be caught in a seam.*

¼" seam
allowance

M

B

¼" seam
allowance

¼" seam allowance

J

*Align arrows with lengthwise
or crosswise grain of fabric.*

K and K reversed

¼" seam allowance

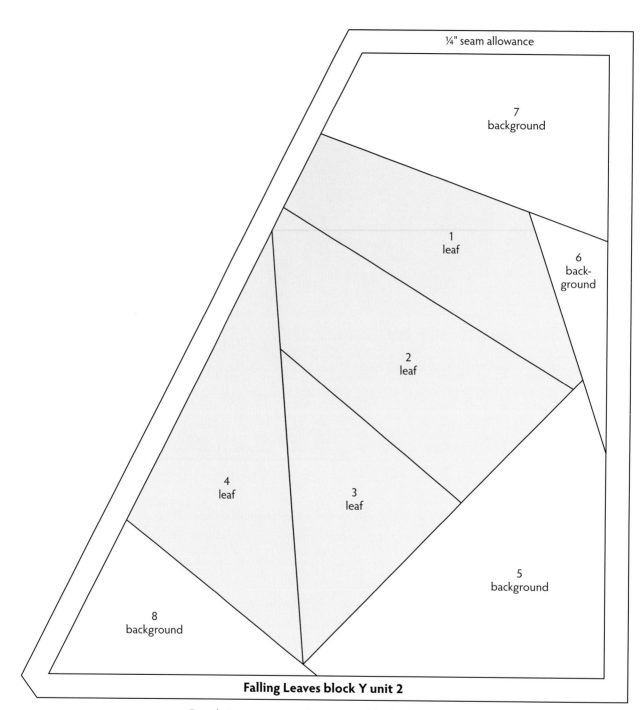

¼" seam allowance

7
background

1
leaf

6
back-
ground

2
leaf

4
leaf

3
leaf

5
background

8
background

Falling Leaves block Y unit 2

Foundation patterns are the reverse of the finished block.

Caroline has always loved the English Ivy design and wanted to create her own variation of the proud and sturdy motif with this quilt. While the overall look of this quilt is scrappy, each block has controlled elements. For each block, you'll need two different assorted batiks for the flower, plus one light-green and one dark-green batik for the leaves.

Designed and sewn by Caroline Reardon, former *Quiltmaker* editor; quilted by Donna Smith.

Finished Quilt: 65" x 84½"
Finished Blocks: 9" x 9"

Materials

Yardage is based on 42"-wide fabric. Although fabric amounts for foundation piecing are adequate, you may need more if you cut very generous pieces.

6⅞ yards of cream tone-on-tone print for blocks, sashing, setting triangles, bottom border, and binding

1½ yards *total* of assorted batiks for blocks

1 yard *total* of assorted dark-green batiks for blocks

⅞ yard *total* of assorted light-green batiks for blocks

¼ yard of dark-green batik for flower stems

¼ yard of gold tone-on-tone print for sashing squares

5⅝ yards of backing fabric

74" x 93" piece of batting

Cutting

Each block uses the same batik for two pieces in the flower-center unit and three A squares. Each block also uses one light-green and one dark-green batik for the leaves. Repeat the cutting instructions to make 31 blocks. When cutting the cream fabric, cut the biggest pieces first.

FOR EACH BLOCK

From the assorted batiks, cut:
3 squares, 2⅜" x 2⅜" (A)
Set aside the remaining fabrics for foundation piecing the flower-center unit.

From the assorted dark-green batiks, cut:
5 squares, 2⅜" x 2⅜" (A)
1 square, 2⅜" x 2⅜"; cut in half diagonally to yield 2 triangles (C)

From the assorted light-green batiks, cut:
3 squares, 2⅜" x 2⅜" (A)
2 squares, 2⅜" x 2⅜"; cut in half diagonally to yield 4 triangles (C)

FOR FLOWER STEMS

From the dark-green batik, cut:
  4 strips, 1" x 42" (F)

FOR BLOCKS, SASHING, SETTING TRIANGLES, BOTTOM BORDER, AND BINDING

From the *lengthwise grain* of the cream tone-on-tone print, cut:
  1 border strip, 4½" x 68"

From the remaining cream tone-on-tone print, cut:
  9 binding strips, 2¼" x 42"
  217 squares, 2⅜" x 2⅜" (A)
  31 squares, 5⅜" x 5⅜"; cut in half diagonally to yield 62 triangles (B)
  31 squares, 2⅜" x 2⅜"; cut in half diagonally to yield 62 triangles (C)
  31 squares, 2" x 2" (D)
  16 squares, 3⅞" x 3⅞"; cut in half diagonally to yield 32 triangles (E) (1 triangle is extra)
  62 rectangles, 2½" x 9½" (G)
  8 rectangles, 2½" x 11½" (H)
  2 rectangles, 2½" x 22½" (J)
  1 rectangle, 2½" x 24½" (K)
  3 squares, 16⅞" x 16⅞"; cut into quarters diagonally to yield 12 triangles (L) (2 triangles are extra)
  2 squares, 17⅞" x 17⅞"; cut in half diagonally to yield 4 triangles (M)

FOR SASHING SQUARES

From the gold tone-on-tone print, cut:
  31 squares, 2½" x 2½" (I)

Making the Blocks

1. Make 31 copies of the foundation pattern on page 30.

2. Referring to "Foundation-Piecing Basics" on page 91, paper piece the flower-center unit in numerical order. Press and trim after adding each piece. Make one for each block (31 total).

Make 1 for
each block.

3. Referring to "Triangle Squares" on page 90 and the unit diagrams, pair up the A squares in the appropriate colors to make units 1–4 as shown. Press the seam allowances toward the darker triangles. Make the number indicated of each unit. (You'll have one unit 1 and one unit 3 left over from each block.)

Unit 1.
Make 6 for
each block.

Unit 2.
Make 6 for
each block.

Unit 3.
Make 4 for
each block.

Unit 4.
Make 2 for
each block.

4. Join five of unit 1, one flower-center unit, and two cream B triangles as shown to make a flower section. Press the seam allowances in the direction indicated.

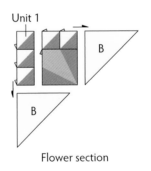

Flower section

5. Join six of unit 2, two of unit 3, two of unit 4, four light-green C triangles, two cream C triangles, one cream D square, and one cream E triangle as shown to make a leaf section. Press the seam allowances in the direction indicated.

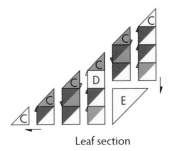

Leaf section

6. To make the flower stems, press the dark-green F strips in half, wrong sides together. Sew using a ¼" seam allowance and press as shown. Cut the strips into 31 pieces, 4¾" long.

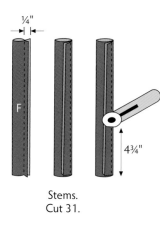

Stems.
Cut 31.

7. Center a stem in the middle of a leaf section as shown. Use matching thread and a blind stitch to appliqué the stem in place.

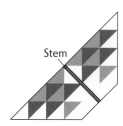

Appliqué stem.

Blind stitch

8. Sew a flower section and a leaf section together as shown. Sew two dark-green C triangles to adjacent sides of the remaining unit 3. Then sew this unit to the bottom of a leaf section to complete the block. Repeat the process to make 31 blocks total.

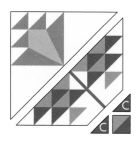

Make 31.

Assembling the Quilt Top

1. Referring to the quilt assembly diagram, join the gold I squares and the cream G rectangles, H rectangles, and J rectangles to make the various sashing rows. Press the seam allowances toward the cream rectangles.

2. Join the blocks and cream G rectangles as shown to make block rows. Then add the sashing rows and the cream K rectangle. Sew cream L triangles to the ends of the rows as shown to make diagonal rows. Press the seam allowances toward the sashing rows.

3. Sew the diagonal rows together, pressing the seam allowances toward the sashing rows. Sew cream M triangles to the corners; press.

4. Referring to "Squared Borders" on page 93, measure, cut, and sew the 68"-long cream border strip to the bottom of the quilt top.

5. Carefully remove the foundation papers.

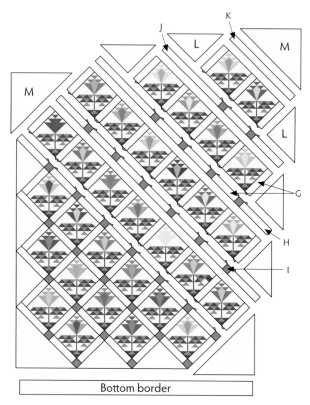

Bottom border

Quilt assembly

Quilting and Finishing

Refer to "Basic Quiltmaking Lessons" on page 89 for more information on quilting and finishing your quilt.

1. Mark the Spring Blooms quilting pattern on pages 30 and 31 in the blocks as shown in the quilting placement diagram.

2. Layer and baste together the backing, batting, and quilt top.

3. Quilt the marked motifs. Quilt a leafy vine in the sashing and setting triangles as shown.

4. Bind the quilt using the cream strips.

Quilting placement

Woolly Petals

Use black flannel and yummy hand-dyed wools to make four wooly flower blocks for this wall quilt. Wool appliqué is a great way to add texture and dimension to your quilting projects! The wools shown are by Weeks Dye Works.

Connect pattern on page 31 along this line.

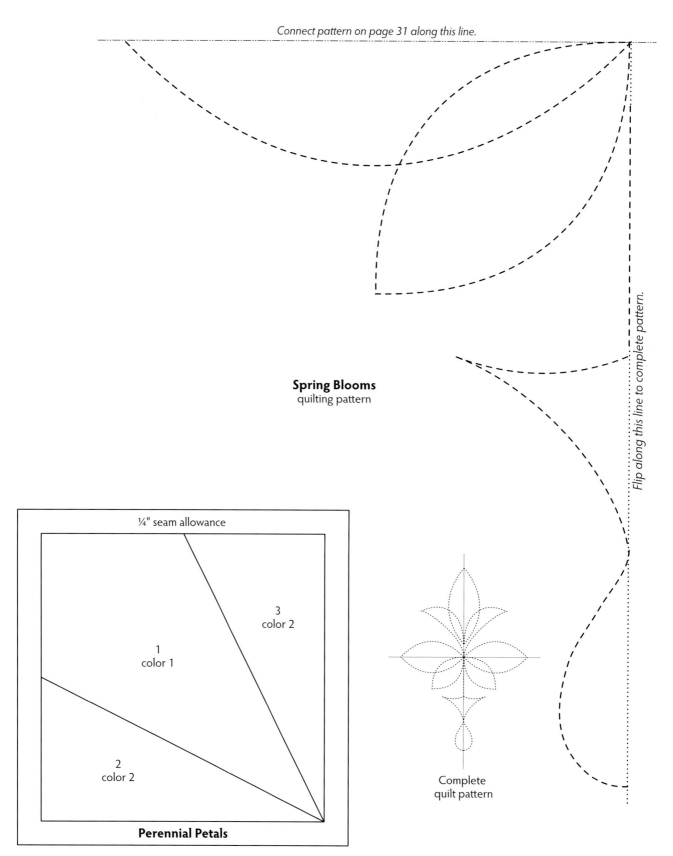

Spring Blooms
quilting pattern

Flip along this line to complete pattern.

¼" seam allowance

3
color 2

1
color 1

2
color 2

Perennial Petals

Complete
quilt pattern

Foundation patterns are the reverse of the finished block.

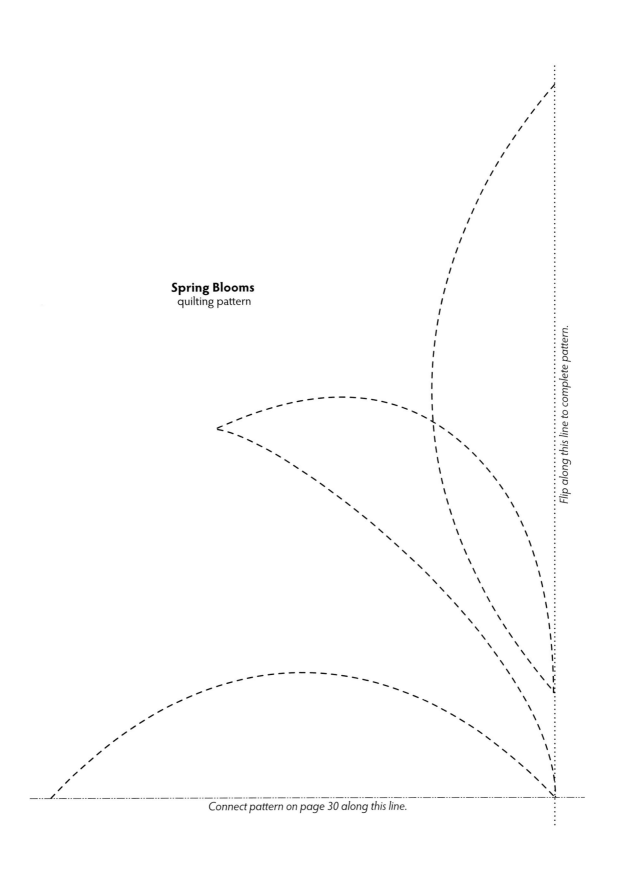

Spring Blooms
quilting pattern

Flip along this line to complete pattern.

Connect pattern on page 30 along this line.

W anting to make a basket quilt for a long time, Carolyn Beam played with different designs and colors in her software program, Electric Quilt, until she came up with one that she liked. Pink and brown is one of Carolyn's favorite color combinations, so this quilt was perfect for taking a huge bite out of her stash!

Designed and sewn by Carolyn Beam, *Quiltmaker* creative editor; quilted by ZJ Humbach.

Finished Quilt: 98" x 98"
Finished Blocks: 10" x 10"

Materials

Yardage is based on 42"-wide fabric unless otherwise noted. Fat quarters are approximately 18" x 20". While the overall look of this quilt is scrappy, each block has controlled elements. For variety in the blocks, be sure to use a wide range of values.

4¾ yards *total* **or** 19 fat quarters of assorted beige prints for blocks

3⅞ yards *total* **or** 16 fat quarters of assorted medium-pink and dark-pink prints for blocks and pieced outer border

3½ yards *total* **or** 14 fat quarters of assorted medium-brown and dark-brown prints for blocks and pieced outer border

1⅜ yards of brown print for inner border and binding

9⅜ yards of backing fabric

107" x 107" piece of batting

Cutting

CUTTING FOR BLOCK X

For each block, cut the following pieces. Repeat the instructions to make 18 blocks.

From the beige print #1, cut:
  1 square, 2½" x 2½" (A)
  1 square, 2⅞" x 2⅞"; cut in half diagonally to yield 2 triangles (B)
  1 square, 5¼" x 5¼"; cut into quarters diagonally to yield 4 triangles (C) (2 triangles are extra)
  1 square, 4⅞" x 4⅞"; cut in half diagonally to yield 2 triangles (D) (1 triangle is extra)
  2 rectangles, 2½" x 6½" (E)

From the beige print #2, cut:
  1 square, 4⅞" x 4⅞"; cut in half diagonally to yield 2 triangles (D) (1 triangle is extra)

From the pink print #1, cut:
  2 squares, 2⅞" x 2⅞"; cut in half diagonally to yield 4 triangles (B)

From the pink print #2, cut:
  1 square, 2⅞" x 2⅞"; cut in half diagonally to yield 2 triangles (B)
  1 square, 4⅞" x 4⅞"; cut in half diagonally to yield 2 triangles (D) (1 triangle is extra)

From the brown print #1, cut:
  3 squares, 2⅞" x 2⅞"; cut in half diagonally to yield 6 triangles (B)

From the brown print #2, cut:
  1 square, 2⅞" x 2⅞"; cut in half diagonally to yield 2 triangles (B)
  1 square, 4⅞" x 4⅞"; cut in half diagonally to yield 2 triangles (D) (1 triangle is extra)

Continued on page 34

CUTTING FOR BLOCK Y

For each block, cut the following pieces. Repeat the instructions to make 18 blocks.

From the beige print #1, cut:
1 square, 2½" x 2½" (A)
1 square, 2⅞" x 2⅞"; cut in half diagonally to yield 2 triangles (B)
1 square, 5¼" x 5¼"; cut into quarters diagonally to yield 4 triangles (C) (2 triangles are extra)
1 square, 4⅞" x 4⅞"; cut in half diagonally to yield 2 triangles (D) (1 triangle is extra)
2 rectangles, 2½" x 6½" (E)

From the beige print #2, cut:
1 square, 4⅞" x 4⅞"; cut in half diagonally to yield 2 triangles (D) (1 triangle is extra)

From the pink print #1, cut:
3 squares, 2⅞" x 2⅞"; cut in half diagonally to yield 6 triangles (B)

From the pink print #2, cut:
1 square, 2⅞" x 2⅞"; cut in half diagonally to yield 2 triangles (B)
1 square, 4⅞" x 4⅞"; cut in half diagonally to yield 2 triangles (D) (1 triangle is extra)

From the brown print #1, cut:
2 squares, 2⅞" x 2⅞"; cut in half diagonally to yield 4 triangles (B)

From the brown print #2, cut:
1 square, 2⅞" x 2⅞"; cut in half diagonally to yield 2 triangles (B)
1 square, 4⅞" x 4⅞"; cut in half diagonally to yield 2 triangles (D) (1 triangle is extra)

CUTTING FOR BLOCK Z

For each block, cut the following pieces. Repeat the instructions to make 25 blocks.

From the beige print #1, cut:
8 squares, 2½" x 2½" (A)

From the beige print #2, cut:
4 squares, 2½" x 2½" (A)

From the pink print #1, cut:
2 squares, 2½" x 2½" (A)

From the pink print #2, cut:
2 squares, 2½" x 2½" (A)

From the pink print #3, cut:
4 squares, 2½" x 2½" (A)

From the brown print #1, cut:
2 squares, 2½" x 2½" (A)

From the brown print #2, cut:
2 squares, 2½" x 2½" (A)

From the brown print #3, cut:
1 square, 2½" x 2½" (A)

CUTTING FOR UNIT 1

For each unit, cut the following pieces. Repeat the instructions to make 10 units.

From the beige print #1, cut:
4 squares, 2½" x 2½" (A)

From the beige print #2, cut:
2 squares, 2½" x 2½" (A)

From the pink print #1, cut:
1 square, 2½" x 2½" (A)

From the pink print #2, cut:
1 square, 2½" x 2½" (A)

From the pink print #3, cut:
2 squares, 2½" x 2½" (A)

From the brown print #1, cut:
2 squares, 2½" x 2½" (A)

From the brown print #2, cut:
2 squares, 2½" x 2½" (A)

From the brown print #3, cut:
1 square, 2½" x 2½" (A)

CUTTING FOR UNIT 2

For each unit, cut the following pieces. Repeat the instructions to make 10 units.

From the beige print #1, cut:
4 squares, 2½" x 2½" (A)

From the beige print #2, cut:
2 squares, 2½" x 2½" (A)

From the pink print #1, cut:
2 squares, 2½" x 2½" (A)

From the pink print #2, cut:
2 squares, 2½" x 2½" (A)

From the pink print #3, cut:
2 squares, 2½" x 2½" (A)

From the brown print #1, cut:
1 square, 2½" x 2½" (A)

From the brown print #2, cut:
1 square, 2½" x 2½" (A)

From the brown print #3, cut:
1 square, 2½" x 2½" (A)

CUTTING FOR UNITS 3 AND 4

For each unit, cut the following pieces. Repeat the instructions to make two of each unit.

From the beige print #1, cut:
2 squares, 2½" x 2½" (A)

From the beige print #2, cut:
1 square, 2½" x 2½" (A)

From the pink print #1, cut:
1 square, 2½" x 2½" (A)

From the pink print #2, cut:
1 square, 2½" x 2½" (A)

From the pink print #3, cut:
1 square, 2½" x 2½" (A)

From the brown print #1, cut:
1 square, 2½" x 2½" (A)

From the brown print #2, cut:
1 square, 2½" x 2½" (A)

From the brown print #3, cut:
1 square, 2½" x 2½" (A)

CUTTING FOR BORDERS AND BINDING

From the assorted medium-pink and dark-pink prints, cut *a total of*:
88 rectangles, 2½" x 5½" (F)

From the assorted medium-brown and dark-brown prints, cut *a total of*:
88 rectangles, 2½" x 5½" (F)
4 squares, 5½" x 5½" (G)

From the brown print, cut:
10 inner-border strips, 2" x 42"
11 binding strips, 2¼" x 42"

Making the Blocks and Units

1. Notice that the only difference between the X and Y blocks is the placement of the pink and brown pieces. Referring to the cutting list and the block piecing diagrams for color-placement guidance, join the pieces to make 18 of block X and 18 of block Y. Press the seam allowances in the direction indicated.

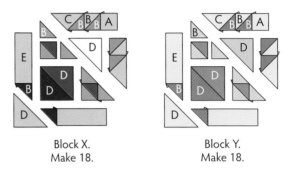

Block X.
Make 18.

Block Y.
Make 18.

2. Notice that pink #3 is the lightest pink in each Z block and in units 1–4. Referring to the cutting list and the block piecing diagrams for color-placement guidance, sew the A squares together as shown to make 25 of block Z. Join the A squares as shown to make 10 of unit 1, 10 of unit 2, and two each of units 3 and 4.

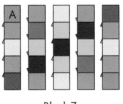

Block Z.
Make 25.

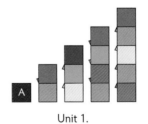

Unit 1.
Make 10.

Unit 2.
Make 10.

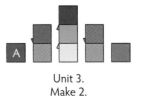

Unit 3.
Make 2.

Unit 4.
Make 2.

Assembling the Quilt Center

1. Lay out the blocks and units in diagonal rows as shown in the quilt assembly diagram, arranging them in a pleasing distribution of color.

2. Join the blocks and units into diagonal rows. Press the seam allowances toward the X and Y blocks.

3. Sew the rows together. Press the seam allowances in one direction.

4. Add units 3 and 4 to the corners and press.

Adding the Borders

1. Align your ruler ¼" beyond the points of the A squares and mark a line on the outside edge of the quilt top. Mark in this way around the entire quilt top.

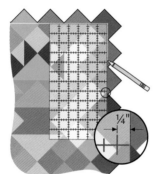

2. Join the 2"-wide brown inner-border strips end to end. Referring to "Squared Borders" on page 93, measure, cut, and sew the strips to the sides of the quilt center, making sure to align the border strips with the marked lines on the quilt top. Trim on the marked lines before pressing the seam allowances toward the border.

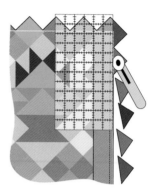

3. In the same way, measure, cut, and sew the brown inner-border strips to the top and bottom of the quilt top to complete the inner border.

4. Randomly join 44 pink and brown F rectangles to make an outer-border strip. Press the seam allowances in one direction. Make four strips.

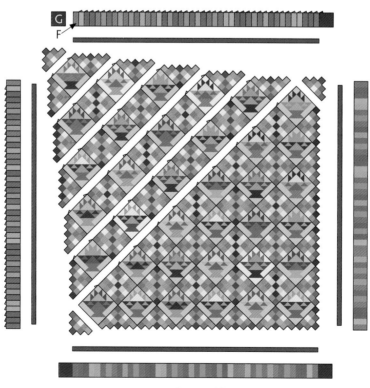

Quilt assembly

5. Matching centers and ends, sew outer-border strips to opposite sides of the quilt. Add brown G squares to both ends of the two remaining strips. Sew these strips to the top and bottom of the quilt top to complete the outer border.

Quilting and Finishing

Refer to "Basic Quiltmaking Lessons" on page 89 for more information on quilting and finishing your quilt.

1. Layer and baste together the backing, batting, and quilt top.

2. Quilt the Paisley Truffles quilting pattern below over the quilt surface as shown in the quilting placement diagram.

3. Bind the quilt using the 2¼"-wide brown strips.

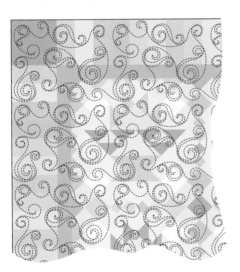

Quilting placement

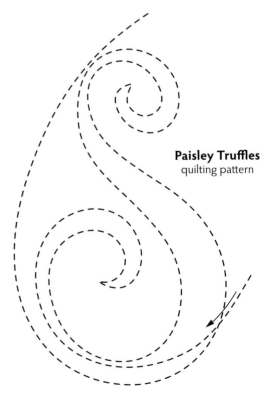

Paisley Truffles
quilting pattern

Arrow indicates direction for continuous-line machine quilting.

iane is always drawn to vintage quilt blocks and found she couldn't pass up a set of 20 blocks for $20. Her non-quilting best friend helped Diane with the layout. It was her friend's idea to layer the smaller Dresden plates on top of the larger ones. What a great result!

Designed and sewn by Diane Harris, *Quiltmaker* interactive editor; quilted by Peg Spradlin.

Finished Quilt: 70½" x 84½"
Finished Blocks: 14" x 14"

Materials

Yardage is based on 42"-wide fabric.

½ yard *each* of 10 assorted gray prints for backgrounds

4 yards *total* of assorted bright prints for Dresden plates

2¼ yards of dark-gray print for border

¼ yard of blue tone-on-tone print for Dresden plate centers

¾ yard of dark-gray tone-on-tone print for binding

5½ yards of backing fabric

79" x 93" piece of batting

19 yards of ½"-wide blue rickrack

Cutting

The B, C, and D patterns are on page 42. The B and C pieces can be cut most easily by first cutting fabric strips in the widths indicated. Lay the template on top of the strip to cut the pieces, rotating the template after each cut. For detailed instructions, refer to "Making Plastic Templates" on page 90 as needed.

From the 10 assorted gray prints, cut *a total of*:
    20 squares, 15½" x 15½" (A)

From the assorted bright prints, cut *a total of*:
    20 strips, 4½" x 42"; cut into 320 B pieces
    16 strips, 2½" x 42"; cut into 512 C pieces

From the blue tone-on-tone print, cut:
    32 D pieces

From the *lengthwise grain* of the dark-gray print, cut:
    4 border strips, 7½" x 73"

From the dark-gray tone-on-tone print, cut:
    2¼"-wide bias-binding strips to total 330"

Making the Blocks

The quilt shown has 18 wedges in the outer rings. We've modified this to 16 wedges for ease in aligning the 16 small wedges over the large ones.

1. Following the diagrams, fold a B piece in half lengthwise with right sides together. Sew across the end using a ¼" seam allowance.

Piecing Tip

Chain sew across the ends of all the B and C pieces, using a very short stitch length. Then trim and turn them in one step. Finally, press all of the pieces.

5. Make 20 large Dresden plates.

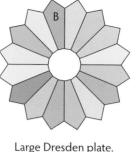

Large Dresden plate.
Make 20.

2. Trim a tiny triangle from the folded seam allowance as shown. Turn the piece right side out and use a stiletto, or other pointed object, to gently push out the point. Press the seam allowances open as shown.

6. Repeat steps 1 and 2 to make 512 C wedges. Join 16 C wedges to make a small Dresden plate. Make 32.

7. Prepare the blue D pieces for "Turned-Edge Appliqué" as described on page 92. Appliqué a D piece in the center of each small Dresden plate using a blind stitch.

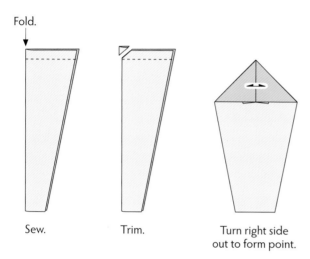

Fold.

Sew. Trim. Turn right side out to form point.

Blind stitch

3. Repeat with all of the B pieces to make 320 wedges.

4. Join 16 B wedges as shown to make a large Dresden plate. Press the seam allowances open.

Small Dresden plate.
Make 32.

8. Appliqué each large Dresden plate to an A square using a blind stitch. Then appliqué a small Dresden plate in the center of each large Dresden plate and press.

9. Center the design and trim each block to measure 14½" x 14½". Make 20 blocks.

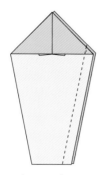

Join wedges.

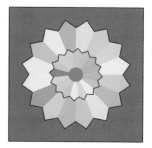

Make 20.

Assembling the Quilt Top

1. Use a design wall to arrange the blocks in five rows of four blocks each. When you're pleased with the arrangement, join the blocks into rows. Press the seam allowances to one side.

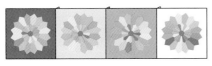

Make 5.

2. Cut 15 pieces of rickrack, each about 12" long. Using thread to match the rickrack, sew a piece of rickrack over the seam lines in each row (the rickrack will be shorter than the seam line as shown). *Note:* We recommend preshrinking the rickrack if it's cotton.

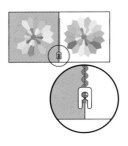

3. Sew the rows together. Cut four pieces of rickrack, each about 57" long. Sew a piece of rickrack over each seam line between the rows.

4. Referring to the photo on page 39, appliqué a small Dresden plate at each seam intersection of four blocks, covering the raw ends of the rickrack.

5. Referring to "Squared Borders" on page 93, measure, cut, and sew the 73"-long dark-gray border strips to the sides, top, and bottom of the quilt center.

6. Cut a 254"-long piece of rickrack. Beginning in the middle of a block, sew the rickrack over the seam line between the blocks and border as shown in the quilt photo, folding the rickrack as you turn each corner. Turn one raw end of the rickrack under about ½" and use it to cover the other raw end.

Quilting and Finishing

Refer to "Basic Quiltmaking Lessons" on page 89 for more information on quilting and finishing your quilt.

1. Layer and baste together the backing, batting, and quilt top.

2. Referring to the quilting placement diagram, quilt the large and small Dresden plates and the center circles in the ditch. Add a line of echo quilting to the Dresden plates as shown. Quilt straight lines on both sides of the rickrack. Quilt free-form loops in the border.

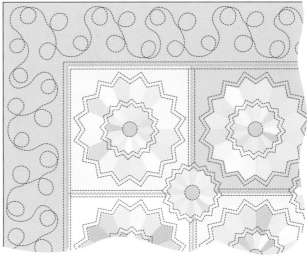

Quilting placement

3. Use the corner-scallop and side-scallop patterns on page 42 to mark the border as shown, matching the dots and reversing every other side scallop.

4. Slide a cutting mat under the quilt and use a small rotary cutter to cut the scallops as marked, moving the mat as needed.

5. Bind the quilt using the dark-gray bias strips.

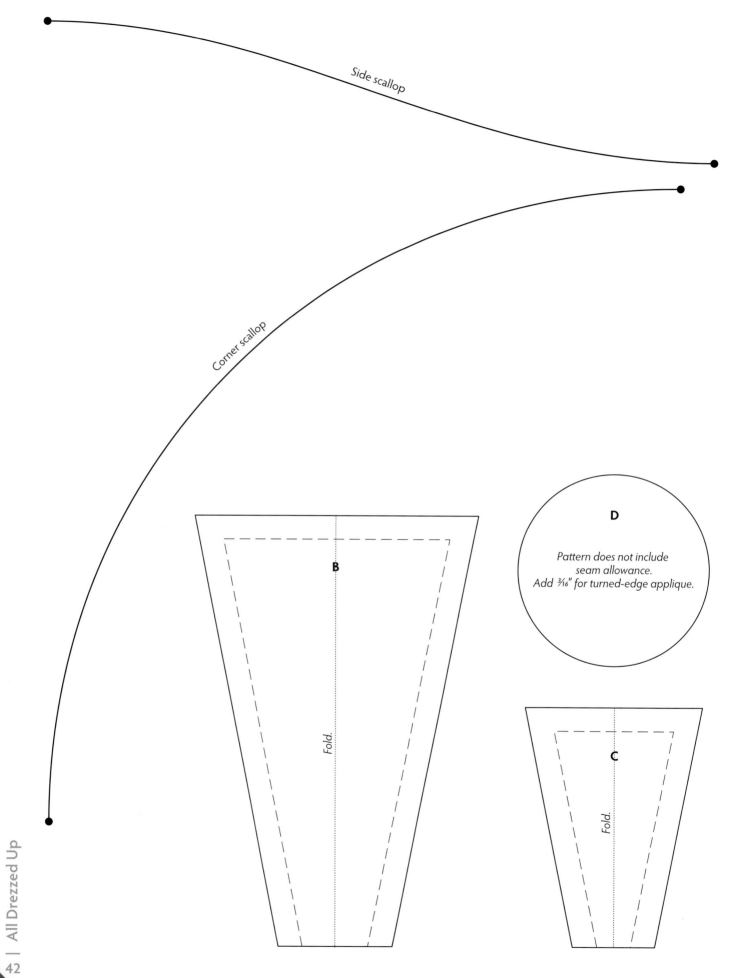

Side scallop

Corner scallop

B

Fold.

D

*Pattern does not include
seam allowance.
Add ³⁄₁₆" for turned-edge applique.*

C

Fold.

Elegant hand-dyed solids from Cherrywood Fabrics play up a simple design, giving this quilt the feel of an Amish quilt. The feather quilting motifs, designed by Theresa Eisinger just for this quilt, alternate between being thick and thin, for a unique spin on traditional feathered quilting.

Designed by Diane Harris, *Quiltmaker* interactive editor; made by Peg Spradlin.

Finished Quilt: 52½" x 70½"
Finished Blocks: 10" x 10"

Materials

Yardage is based on 42"-wide fabric.

2 yards of blue-violet hand-dyed solid fabric for blocks and sashing

2 yards of royal-blue hand-dyed solid fabric for border and binding

⅔ yard of bright-teal hand-dyed solid fabric for blocks

⅔ yard of navy-blue hand-dyed solid fabric for blocks

⅔ yard *total* of assorted green and gold hand-dyed solid fabrics for blocks

½ yard of light-green hand-dyed solid fabric for blocks

⅓ yard of purple hand-dyed solid fabric for blocks

3⅝ yards of backing fabric

61" x 79" piece of batting

Cutting

From the *lengthwise grain* of the blue-violet hand-dyed solid fabric, cut:
    4 sashing strips, 3½" x 63"
    36 squares, 2¼" x 2¼" (A)

From the light-green hand-dyed solid fabric, cut:
    36 squares, 2¼" x 2¼" (A)
    18 squares, 3¾" x 3¾"; cut into quarters
        diagonally to yield 72 triangles (B)

From the purple hand-dyed solid fabric, cut:
    18 squares, 3¾" x 3¾"; cut into quarters
        diagonally to yield 72 triangles (B)

From the bright-teal hand-dyed solid fabric, cut:
    18 squares, 6¼" x 6¼"; cut into quarters
        diagonally to yield 72 triangles (C)

From the navy-blue hand-dyed solid fabric, cut:
    18 squares, 6¼" x 6¼"; cut into quarters
        diagonally to yield 72 triangles (C)

From the assorted green and gold hand-dyed solid fabrics, cut *a total of*:
    18 squares, 6¼" x 6¼"; cut into quarters
        diagonally to yield 72 triangles (C)

From the *lengthwise grain* of the royal-blue hand-dyed solid, cut:
    2 border strips, 5½" x 63"
    2 border strips, 5½" x 55"
    5 binding strips, 2¼" x 54"

Making the Blocks

Press the seam allowances in the direction indicated.

1. Lay out pieces A–C as shown in the diagram following step 3, using the assorted green and gold C triangles in the positions marked with an asterisk.

2. Join the A squares to make a four-patch unit. Join the B triangles to make a pieced-triangle unit. Join the pieced-triangle unit to the four-patch unit; then add bright-teal C triangles to make the center unit.

3. Join the navy-blue C triangles to the green/gold triangles to make corner triangles. Join the corner triangles to the center unit to complete the block. Repeat the process to make 18 blocks total.

Make 18.

Assembling the Quilt Top

1. Paying attention to the block orientation, join six blocks to make a vertical row as shown in the quilt assembly diagram. Make three vertical rows.

2. Join the rows with the blue-violet sashing strips, trimming any extra length from the sashing.

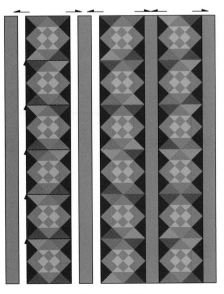

Quilt assembly

3. Referring to "Squared Borders" on page 93, measure, cut, and sew the 63"-long royal-blue strips to the sides of the quilt top. Then add the 55"-long royal-blue strips to the top and bottom of the quilt top to complete the outer border.

Quilting and Finishing

Refer to "Basic Quiltmaking Lessons" on page 89 for more information on quilting and finishing your quilt.

1. Mark the Sea Swish quilting pattern on page 46 in the sashing. Mark the Fluctuating Feathers quilting pattern on page 46 in the outer border, matching the dots and reversing every other motif as shown in red. Notice that each motif can be quilted continuously.

Quilting placement

2. Layer and baste together the backing, batting, and quilt top.

3. Quilt the rows and sashing in the ditch. Add outline quilting in the sashing. Using the patchwork as a guide, quilt diagonal lines in the blocks as shown in the quilting placement diagram. Quilt the marked motifs.

4. Bind the quilt using the royal-blue strips.

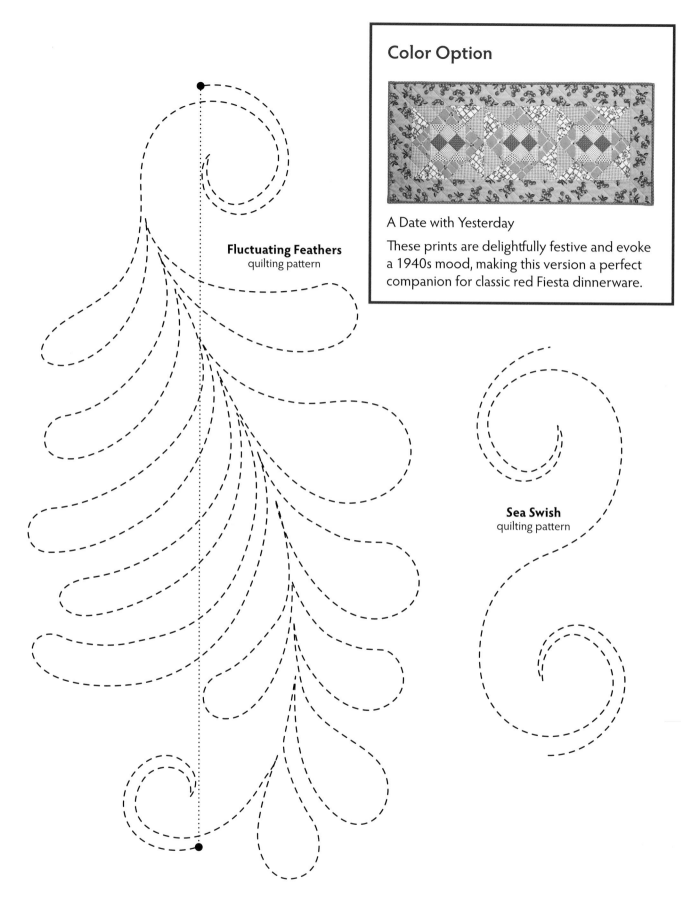

Fluctuating Feathers
quilting pattern

Sea Swish
quilting pattern

Color Option

A Date with Yesterday

These prints are delightfully festive and evoke a 1940s mood, making this version a perfect companion for classic red Fiesta dinnerware.

Y ou don't need a green thumb to plant this scrappy little garden. Tiny flowers are foundation pieced in a unique, new way and embellished with petite buttons. The seam lines are really just guidelines—you can skip a few or add one or two extra, and still have natural-looking petals. A variety of medium-green fabrics will add more interest to the quilt. We arranged the lightest of the patches and blocks near the top of the quilt and used the darkest toward the bottom. Follow Mother Nature's lead and improvise.

Designed by Theresa Eisinger, former *Quiltmaker* graphic designer; pieced by Theresa Spradlin and Peg Spradlin; quilted by Peg Spradlin.

Finished Quilt: 18½" x 21½"
Finished Blocks: 1½" x 1½", 3" x 3", and 6" x 6"

Materials

Yardage is based on 42"-wide fabric unless otherwise noted. Although fabric amounts for foundation piecing are adequate, you may need more if you cut very generous pieces.

1⅜ yards *total* of assorted medium-green prints for blocks, border, and binding

½ yard *total* of assorted white prints for blocks

½ yard *total* of assorted pink prints for blocks

Continued on page 48

10" x 10" square of blue tone-on-tone print for watering-can block

¾ yard of backing fabric

23" x 26" piece of batting

10 pink buttons, ⅝" to ¾" diameter, for pink flower centers

25 yellow buttons, ⅜" diameter, for white flower centers

Small beads for embellishment

Cutting

From the assorted medium-green prints, cut *a total of*:

39 squares, 2" x 2" (A)
12 border rectangles, 2" x 8"
Random lengths of 2¼"-wide binding strips to total 88"

From the blue tone-on-tone print, cut:

1 bias strip, 1" x 7" (watering-can handle)

Making the Blocks

The foundation patterns are on page 51. Refer to "Foundation-Piecing Basics" on page 91 for detailed instructions as needed.

1. Make one copy of the watering-can foundation pattern. Make 25 copies of the white-flower foundation pattern and 10 copies of the pink-flower foundation pattern.

2. Paper piece the watering can in numerical order, leaving the small areas between the dots unstitched. Press and trim after adding each piece. The bias-strip handle will be inserted in the seam openings in step 3 of "Assembling the Quilt Top."

Watering can.
Make 1.

3. Before paper piecing the flowers, use scissors to cut along the bold line on the flower patterns from the paper's edge to the center; then cut out the center circles.

4. Paper piece the flowers in numerical order. Press and trim after adding each piece. To reduce bulk, trim the seam allowances to 1/16". Notice in the photo on page 47 that some of the flowers were made with fewer petals. We used the stitching lines as a guide for a more improvisational approach to paper piecing the flowers.

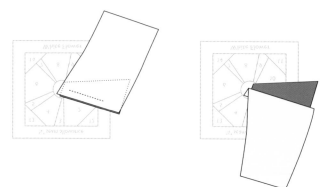

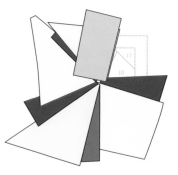

5. Before adding the green corner pieces, fold back the foundation at the cut line. With right sides together, match the raw edges of the first and last pieces and sew them together.

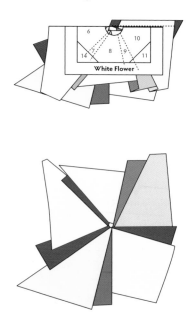

6. Finish the block by adding the green corner pieces. (The center circle remains unstitched; it will be covered later with a button.)

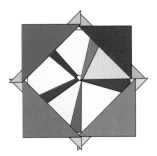

7. Repeat steps 4–6 to make 25 white flowers and 10 pink flowers. Trim the blocks along the outer line to remove excess fabric and paper.

White flower.
Make 25.

Pink flower.
Make 10.

Assembling the Quilt Top

1. Referring to the quilt assembly diagram, sew the blocks and green A squares into sections as shown. Press the seam allowances in the direction indicated. Sew the sections together and press.

Quilt assembly

2. Gently remove the foundation papers.

3. Refer to "Bias Strips" on page 93 to make the watering-can handle. Insert the ends of the bias strip into the seam openings of the block and pin in place. Use matching thread and a blind stitch to appliqué the handle to the background. Sew the openings closed.

Blind stitch

4. Arrange the green border rectangles from the lightest value to the darkest value; join the rectangles end to end.

5. Cut this strip into four 21"-long strips. Set aside the lightest-value strip for the top border and the darkest-value strip for the bottom border. Referring to "Squared Borders" on page 93, measure, cut, and sew the remaining two strips to opposite sides of the quilt with the lightest-value fabrics at the top. Add the top and bottom strips in the same way to complete the outer border.

Quilting and Finishing

Refer to "Basic Quiltmaking Lessons" on page 89 for more information on quilting and finishing your quilt.

1. Layer and baste together the backing, batting, and quilt top.

2. Stitch in the ditch around the watering can. Stitch a few lines from the watering-can spout to resemble water spray.

3. Refer to the quilting placement diagram and quilt around the flower petals as shown. Using the quilting pattern below, stitch free-form leaves in the green squares, connecting the leaves with curved lines.

Quilting placement

4. Join enough 2¼"-wide green strips of random lengths end to end to make one 88"-long continuous binding strip. Note that the binding strips are also joined from light to dark value. Bind the quilt using the green binding strip.

5. Add the buttons to the flower centers. Add the small beads randomly to resemble dewdrops and along the quilted lines from the watering-can spout.

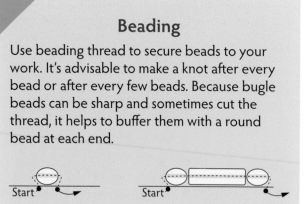

Beading

Use beading thread to secure beads to your work. It's advisable to make a knot after every bead or after every few beads. Because bugle beads can be sharp and sometimes cut the thread, it helps to buffer them with a round bead at each end.

Start   Single bead   Start   Bugle bead

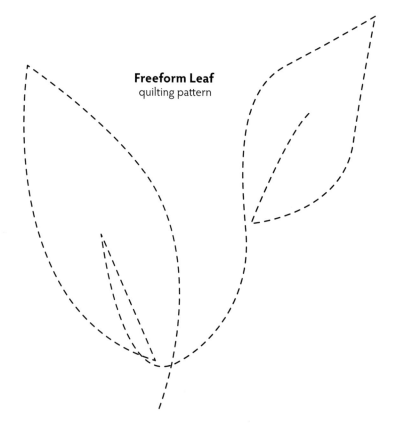

Freeform Leaf
quilting pattern

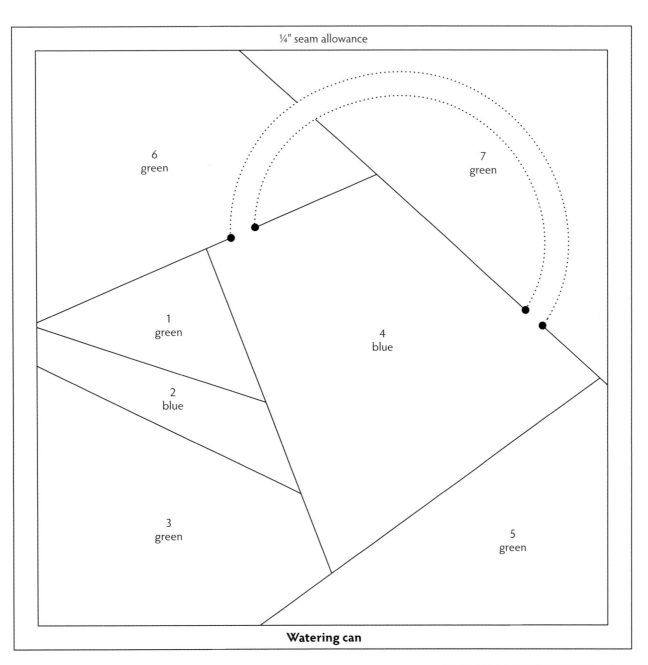

¼" seam allowance

6
green

7
green

1
green

4
blue

2
blue

3
green

5
green

Watering can

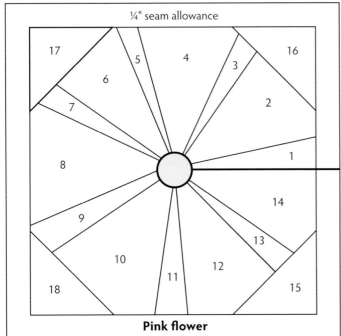

¼" seam allowance

17

5

4

16

6

3

7

2

8

1

9

14

10

13

11

12

15

18

Pink flower

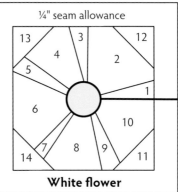

¼" seam allowance

13

3

12

4

2

5

1

6

10

7

8

9

11

14

White flower

Foundation patterns are
the reverse of the finished blocks.

June wanted to showcase sun-dyed fabrics from Langa Lapu, a South African company, so she created this simple design in which the lush ferns, leaves, and other natural elements of the fabrics take center stage.

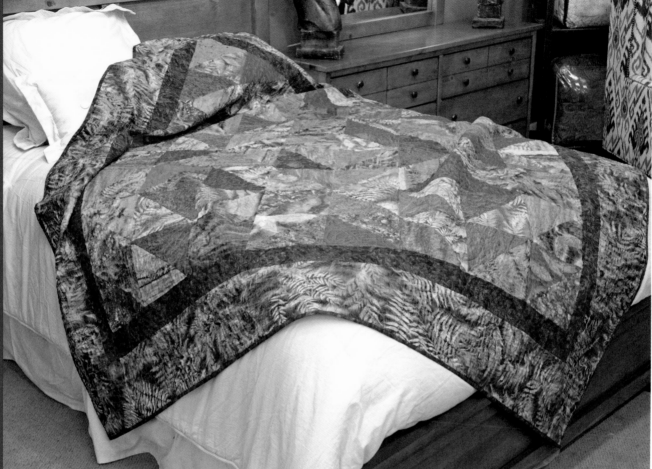

Designed and sewn by June Dudley, *Quiltmaker* editor in chief; quilted by Peg Spradlin.

Finished Quilt: 86½" x 86½"
Finished Blocks: 8" x 8"

Materials

Yardage is based on 42"-wide fabric.

2¾ yards of multicolored print for outer border

⅓ yard *each* of 8 assorted yellow-green, green, and blue-green prints for blocks

⅓ yard *each* of 8 assorted blue, blue-violet, violet, and red-violet prints for blocks

2¼ yards of purple tone-on-tone print for inner border and binding

8⅓ yards of backing fabric

95" x 95" piece of batting

Cutting

From *each* of the assorted yellow-green, green, and blue-green prints, cut:
  4 squares, 8⅞" x 8⅞" (A)

From *each* of the assorted blue, blue-violet, violet, and red-violet prints, cut:
  4 squares, 8⅞" x 8⅞" (A)

From the *lengthwise grain* of the purple tone-on-tone print, cut:
  2 inner-border strips, 3½" x 67"
  2 inner-border strips, 3½" x 73"
  6 binding strips, 2¼" x 62"

From the *lengthwise grain* of the multicolored print, cut:
  2 outer-border strips, 8½" x 73"
  2 outer-border strips, 8½" x 89"

Making the Blocks

1. Referring to "Triangle Squares" on page 90, pair a green A square with a blue A square to make two triangle-square units. Repeat to make a total of 64 units.

Make 64.

Design Tip
It may be helpful to lay out the blocks on a design wall or the floor before sewing the units together.

2. Noting the placement of the greens and blues in the assembly diagram, lay out 16 units, placing less-distinct colors around the edges of the block. Sew the units together into rows. Press the seam allowances in the directions indicated. Sew the rows together and press. Make four blocks.

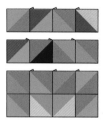 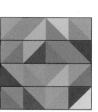

Make 4.

About the Colors

The colors in these sun-dyed fabrics are analogous; they're next to each other on the color wheel, and range from yellow-green to red-violet. Each block is made from a green fabric and a blue or violet fabric; we'll just refer to them as green and blue throughout the pattern. It may not always be obvious if a specific blue-green should go in the green pile or the blue pile. Lay it next to the other colors and let them help you decide which color is more prominent.

Assembling the Quilt Top

1. Arrange the blocks in two rows of two blocks each. Sew the blocks together into rows; press. Sew the rows together and press the seam allowances to one side.

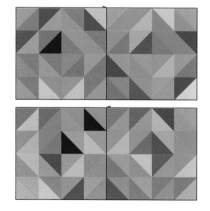

Quilt assembly

2. Referring to "Squared Borders" on page 93, measure, cut, and sew the 67"-long purple inner-border strips to the sides of the quilt top. Then add the 73"-long purple inner-border strips to the top and bottom of the quilt top in the same way.

3. Measure, cut, and sew the 73"-long multicolored outer-border strips to the sides of the quilt top. Add the 89"-long multicolored outer-border strips to the top and bottom of the quilt top.

Quilting and Finishing

Refer to "Basic Quiltmaking Lessons" on page 89 for more information on quilting and finishing your quilt.

1. Layer and baste together the backing, batting, and quilt top.

2. This is a perfect quilt for free-motion quilting. See "Free-Motion Quilting" on page 94 if this is new for you. Referring to the Curly Frond quilting pattern on page 55, mark spines in the blocks and borders as shown in the quilting placement diagram. Notice that the motifs shown in red are reversed. Adjust the spine in the corners of the inner border as shown in brown. Any household object about 8" in diameter can be used to mark the spines. Using the marked spines as a guide, quilt the ferns freehand. Peg quilted an echo line around each fern, adding tendrils as shown in green.

3. Bind the quilt using the purple strips.

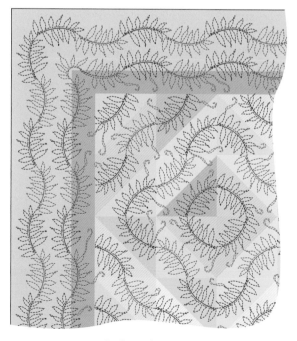

Quilting placement

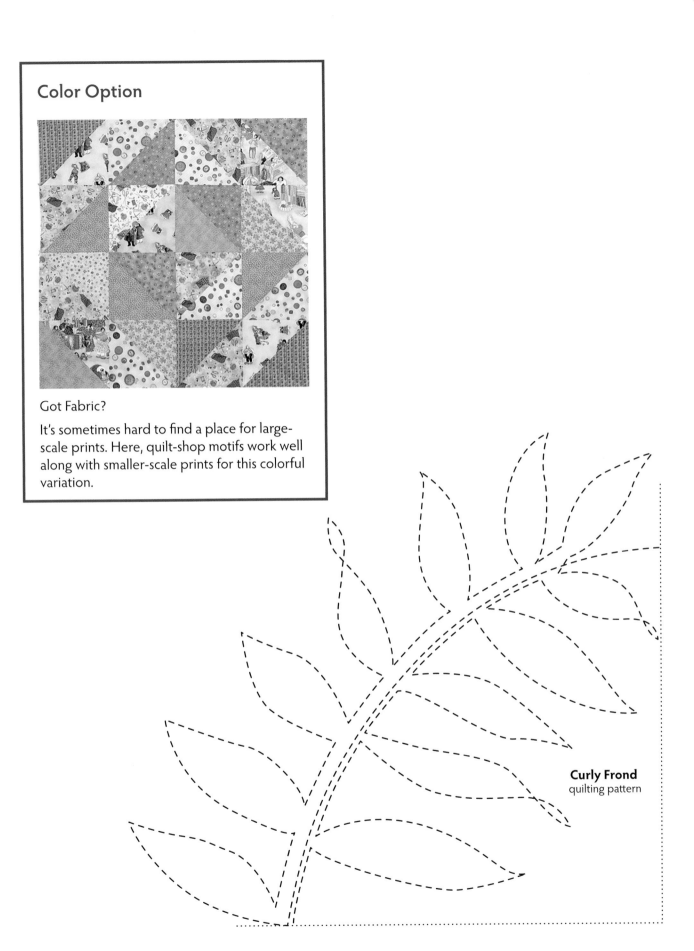

Color Option

Got Fabric?

It's sometimes hard to find a place for large-scale prints. Here, quilt-shop motifs work well along with smaller-scale prints for this colorful variation.

Curly Frond
quilting pattern

Carolyn designed this quilt to use Pinwheel blocks acquired through a block exchange with coworkers. Her design creates the effect of a pinwheel inside a pinwheel. If you'd like to exchange blocks with quilting friends, choose an easy-to-sew block and set a reasonable time frame for completing the blocks.

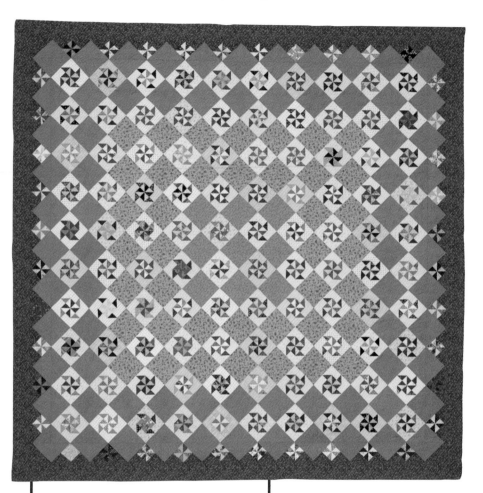

Designed and sewn by Carolyn Beam, *Quiltmaker* creative editor; quilted by ZJ Humbach.

Finished Quilt: 102½" x 102½"
Finished Blocks: 6" x 6"

Materials

Yardage is based on 42"-wide fabric.

3⅓ yards *total* of assorted light shirtings for blocks

2¼ yards *total* of assorted medium and dark prints for blocks

1⅓ yards *total* of assorted light prints for blocks

3⅓ yards of red print for setting triangles, border, and binding

2⅜ yards of blue print #1 for setting squares

1½ yards of blue print #2 for setting squares

½ yard of blue print #3 for setting squares

9¾ yards of backing fabric

111" x 111" piece of batting

Cutting

From the assorted light prints, cut *a total of*:
280 squares, 2⅜" x 2⅜" (A)

From the assorted medium and dark prints, cut *a total of*:
480 squares, 2⅜" x 2⅜" (A)

From the assorted light shirtings, cut *a total of*:*
200 squares, 2⅜" x 2⅜" (A)
400 squares, 2" x 2" (B)
200 rectangles, 2" x 3½" (C)

From the *lengthwise grain* of the red print, cut:
2 border strips, 4¾" x 96"
2 border strips, 4¾" x 105"
5 binding strips, 2¼" x 87"
20 squares, 5½" x 5½"; cut into quarters
    diagonally to yield 80 triangles (D)
2 squares, 5⅛" x 5⅛"; cut in half diagonally to
    yield 4 triangles (F)

From the blue print #1, cut:
72 squares, 6½" x 6½" (E)

From the blue print #2, cut:
40 squares, 6½" x 6½" (E)

From the blue print #3, cut:
9 squares, 6½" x 6½" (E)

** You'll need 100 matching sets of 2 A squares,
4 B squares, and 2 C rectangles.*

Making the Blocks

Although this quilt is very scrappy, there is some continuity to calm things down. Notice that each block uses the same shirting for its background (two A squares, four B squares, and two C rectangles).

1. Referring to "Triangle Squares" on page 90, pair two matching light A squares with two matching medium/dark A squares to make four of unit 1. Repeat to make a total of 560 of unit 1, keeping matching sets of four units together.

Unit 1.
Make 560.

2. Using unit 1, sew four matching units together to make a pinwheel unit. Make 140 pinwheel units.

Pinwheel unit.
Make 140.

3. Repeat step 1, pairing two matching shirting A squares with two matching medium/dark A squares to make four of unit 2. Repeat to make a total of 400 of unit 2, keeping matching sets of four units together.

Unit 2.
Make 400.

4. Using unit 2, join four matching units, four shirting B squares, two shirting C rectangles, and one pinwheel unit as shown to make a block. Make 100 blocks total.

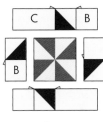

Make 100.

5. Join a pinwheel unit and two red D triangles to make a setting triangle as shown. Make 40 total.

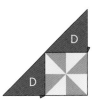

Make 40.

Assembling the Quilt Top

Three different blue prints with similar values are used for the E setting squares and arranged in continuous rings around the center.

1. Paying careful attention to the placement of the blue E squares, join the blocks, setting triangles, and blue E squares into diagonal rows as shown in the quilt assembly diagram. Press the seam allowances toward the blue squares.

2. Sew the rows together and press the seam allowances in one direction. Add a red F triangle to each corner.

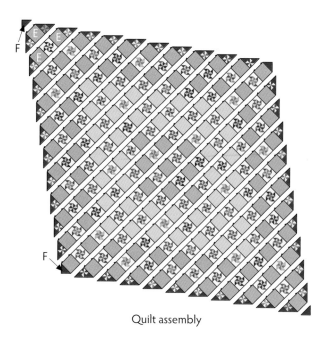

Quilt assembly

3. Referring to "Squared Borders" on page 93, measure, cut, and sew the 96"-long red outer-border strips to the sides of the quilt top. Then add the 105"-long red outer-border strips to the top and bottom of the quilt top.

Quilting and Finishing

Refer to "Basic Quiltmaking Lessons" on page 89 for more information on quilting and finishing your quilt.

1. Mark the Spinning Flowers quilting pattern on page 59 in the blocks, E squares, setting triangles, and border; add partial motifs in the border as shown in the quilting placement diagram.

2. Layer and baste together the backing, batting, and quilt top.

3. Quilt the marked motifs.

4. Bind the quilt using the red strips.

Quilting placement

Color Option

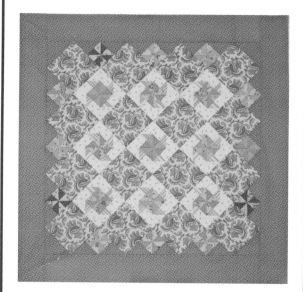

Spin Blown

Softer colors create a charming crib quilt. Color placement in this version is more controlled. The pattern for Spin Blown can be found on the quiltmaker.com website.

Spinning Flowers
quilting pattern

Brightly colored solid fabrics take center stage in these large blocks. They're set off nicely by batik Pinwheel blocks that Theresa received in a block exchange. Notice how the dark-blue and dark-teal fabrics give this quilt the illusion of depth—the stars seem to pop off the surface!

Designed by Theresa Eisinger, former *Quiltmaker* graphic designer; made by Theresa Eisinger and Peg Spradlin.

Finished Quilt: 49¾" x 49¾"
Finished Blocks: 14½" x 14½"

Materials

Yardage is based on 42"-wide fabric.

1⅜ yards *total* of assorted batiks for blocks

⅛ yard *each* of 9 assorted bright-colored solid fabrics for blocks

1⅛ yards of dark-teal solid fabric for blocks and outer border

1⅛ yards of dark-blue tone-on-tone print for blocks and inner border

¾ yard of multicolored batik for inner border and binding

3⅜ yards of backing fabric

57" x 57" piece of batting

Cutting

Each pinwheel unit uses two matching A squares each from two contrasting batiks. Each block uses eight pinwheel units and eight matching B pieces.

From the assorted batiks, cut *a total of*:
288 squares, 2⅜" x 2⅜" (A)

From *each* of the assorted solid fabrics, cut:*
1 strip, 2⅝" x 42"

From the dark-teal solid fabric, cut:*
36 rectangles, 2⅝" x 8½" (C)
4 rectangles, 2⅞" x 21½" (F)

From the dark-blue tone-on-tone print, cut:*
36 rectangles, 2⅝" x 8½" (C)
4 rectangles, 2⅞" x 18" (D)
4 rectangles, 2⅞" x 18" (E)

From the multicolored batik, cut:
6 inner-border strips, 1" x 42"
6 binding strips, 2¼" x 42"

* *See diagrams in steps 2 and 3 of "Making the Blocks" and step 3 of "Assembling the Quilt Top" for further cutting instructions.*

Making the Blocks

The blocks are assembled with Y-seams. Refer to "Triangle Squares" on page 90 for detailed instructions as needed.

1. Using matching A squares from two contrasting batiks, pair each A square with a contrasting A square to make four matching triangle-square units. Sew the matching triangle-square units together as shown to make a pinwheel unit. Repeat to make 72 pinwheel units total.

Pinwheel unit.
Make 72.

2. To cut the B pieces, use the 45° line on a ruler to make the first cut on a 2⅝"-wide solid strip as shown. Continue cutting the strip at 2⅝" intervals to make 8 B pieces. Repeat to cut 8 B pieces from each solid strip (72 total).

Cut 9 matching sets of 8 B pieces.

3. Referring to the diagram, cut off the corners of a C rectangle as shown. Repeat to trim all the dark-teal and dark-blue C rectangles.

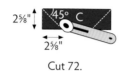

Cut 72.

4. On the wrong side of the pinwheel units, B pieces, and C pieces, use a ruler to mark a ¼" seam allowance in all corners as shown.

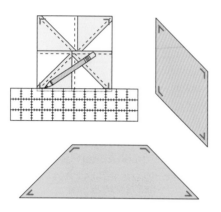

5. Align a pinwheel unit and a B piece right sides together and pin through the ¼" marks on both pieces as shown. Sew seam 1 between the ¼" marks in the direction indicated by the arrow, beginning and ending with a backstitch to secure the seam. Press the seam allowances open.

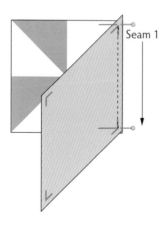

6. Add a second B piece in the same way, sewing in the direction indicated by the arrow at seam 2. Sew seam 3 between the two B pieces in the same way. Add another pinwheel unit, a dark-blue C piece, and a teal C piece in the same way to complete a quadrant as shown. Press the seam allowances open after sewing each seam. Make 36 quadrants.

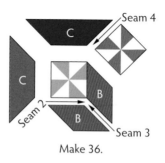

Make 36.

7. Sew four quadrants with matching B pieces together as shown to complete the block. Make nine blocks total.

Make 9.

Assembling the Quilt Top

Use a design wall to arrange the blocks for a pleasing distribution of color.

1. Lay out the blocks in three rows of three blocks each as shown in the quilt assembly diagram. When you're pleased with the arrangement, join the blocks into rows. Press the seam allowances in the direction indicated. Sew the rows together and press.

2. Join the inner-border strips end to end and cut four 47"-long strips.

3. Referring to the diagrams, cut off the corners of the dark-blue D and E rectangles and the dark-teal F rectangles as shown.

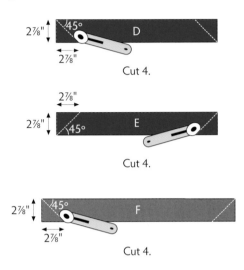

Cut 4.

Cut 4.

Cut 4.

4. Sew dark-blue D and E pieces to a dark-teal F piece as shown in the border unit diagram to make an outer-border strip. Make four strips.

5. Matching the centers, join an inner-border strip to an outer-border strip to make a border unit. Trim the ends of the inner-border strip at an angle to match the edges of the D and E pieces. Repeat to make four border units.

Border unit.
Make 4.

6. Matching the centers and ends, sew the border units to the quilt, starting and stopping ¼" from the edges of the quilt with a backstitch.

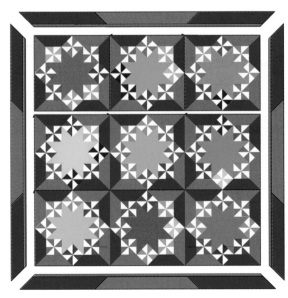

Quilt assembly

7. Miter the corners. Trim the seam allowances to ¼" and press them open.

Quilting and Finishing

Refer to "Basic Quiltmaking Lessons" on page 89 for more information on quilting and finishing your quilt.

1. Refer to the quilting placement diagram below and the quilting patterns on page 64. Mark the Plume 1 quilting pattern in the B pieces, using one curlicue in the center of the block as shown. Mark the Plume 2 quilting pattern in the pinwheel units as shown. Mark the Plume 3 quilting pattern without the red lines in the dark-teal C pieces, and the reverse of the same motif in the dark-blue C pieces as shown. Mark the Plume 3 quilting pattern, without the green lines, in the outer border, reversing every other motif as shown.

2. Layer and baste together the backing, batting, and quilt top.

3. Quilt the marked motifs. Quilt gentle curved lines in the pinwheel units as shown. Quilt the inner border in the ditch. Referring to the detailed photo on page 61, quilt a tiny stipple in the spaces in the block as shown.

4. Bind the quilt using the multicolored-batik strips.

Quilting placement

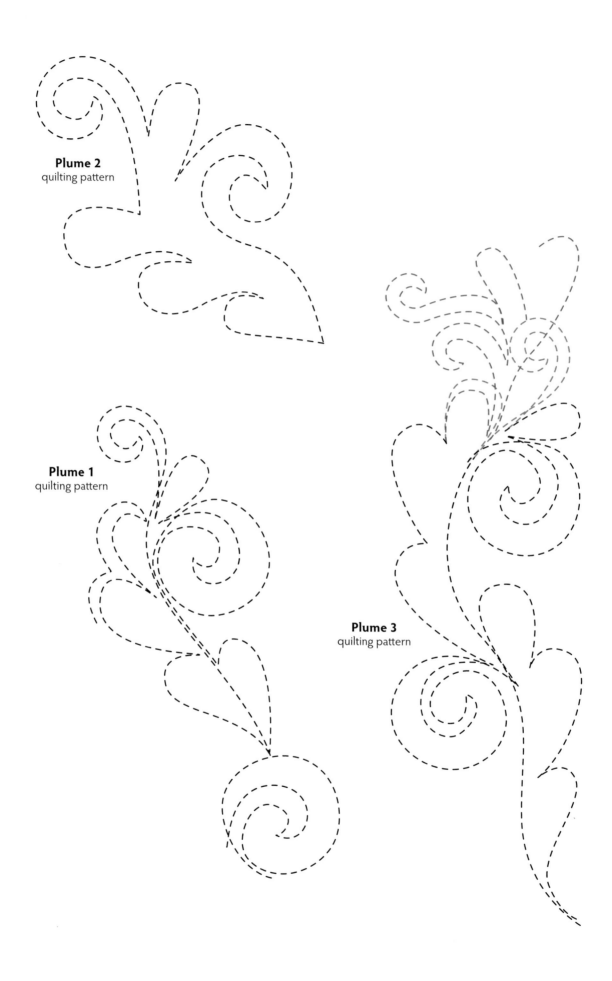

Plume 2
quilting pattern

Plume 1
quilting pattern

Plume 3
quilting pattern

E ileen has a passion for color—but there is so little of it in the frigid winter in Colorado, where she lives. Sewing these foundation-pieced flowers in soft aqua, pink, and purple batiks was the perfect way to beat the winter blues. You can do the same—pick a variety of pinks and purples for a garden of glorious flowers that will bloom all year.

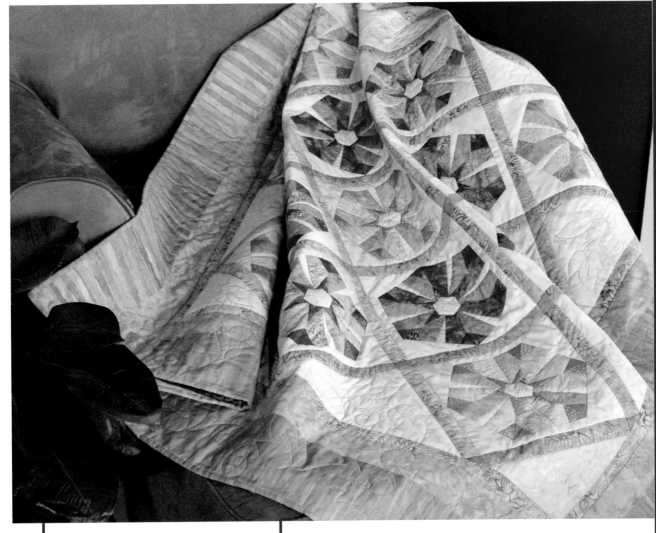

Designed and sewn by Eileen Fowler, *Quiltmaker* associate editor; quilted by Kim Waite.

Finished Quilt: 58½" x 58½"
Finished Blocks: 9" x 9"

Materials

Yardage is based on 42"-wide fabric. Although fabric amounts for foundation piecing are adequate, you may need more if you cut very generous pieces.

2 yards of pale-aqua batik for blocks and setting triangles

1⅞ yards of blue-and-aqua striped batik for outer border and binding

1¼ yards *total* of assorted light- to medium-value pink and purple batiks for blocks and sashing

1¼ yards *total* of assorted dark-value pink and purple batiks for blocks

¾ yard of medium-aqua batik for sashing and inner border

Continued on page 66

⅝ yard of medium-purple batik for middle border

⅜ yard of yellow batik for blocks

4 yards of backing fabric

67" x 67" piece of batting

Cutting

From the pale-aqua batik, cut:
 2 squares, 14" x 14"; cut into quarters diagonally
   to yield 8 triangles (C)
 2 squares, 7¼" x 7¼"; cut in half diagonally to
   yield 4 triangles (D)
 Set aside the remaining fabric for foundation
   piecing.

From 1 of the assorted medium-pink batiks, cut:
 24 squares, 1½" x 1½" (B)
 Set aside the remaining light- to medium-value
   pink and purple batiks for foundation piecing.

From the medium-aqua batik, cut:
 6 inner-border strips, 1½" x 42"
 36 rectangles, 1½" x 9½" (A)

From the medium-purple batik, cut:
 6 middle-border strips, 2¾" x 42"

From the *lengthwise grain* of the blue-and-aqua striped batik, cut:
 4 outer-border strips, 5" x 61"
 5 binding strips, 2¼" x 51"

Making the Blocks

Each flower uses two light- to medium-value batiks and two dark-value batiks in the same color family to give the flowers some added dimension. Refer to "Foundation-Piecing Basics" on page 91 for detailed instructions as needed.

1. Each half of the Flower block is made from three foundation-pieced units. Make 26 copies each of the foundation patterns on pages 68 and 69.

2. Paper piece units 1–3 in numerical order as instructed on the pattern. Press and trim after adding each piece. Make 26 of each unit.

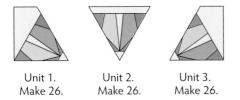

Unit 1.
Make 26.

Unit 2.
Make 26.

Unit 3.
Make 26.

3. Join units 1, 2, and 3 as shown to make a half block. To reduce bulk, press the seam allowances open. Join two half blocks as shown to complete a block; press. Make 13 blocks total.

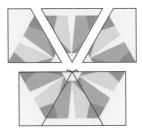

Make 13.

Assembling the Quilt Center

1. Referring to the quilt assembly diagram, join the medium-aqua A rectangles and medium-pink B squares as shown to make sashing rows. Press the seam allowances toward the A rectangles.

2. Join the blocks, medium-aqua A rectangles, and pale-aqua C triangles to make diagonal rows. Press the seam allowances toward the A rectangles.

3. Sew the rows together. Press the seam allowances toward the sashing rows.

4. Add a pale-aqua D triangle to each corner. Trim the B squares even with the edges of the quilt center. Gently remove the foundation papers.

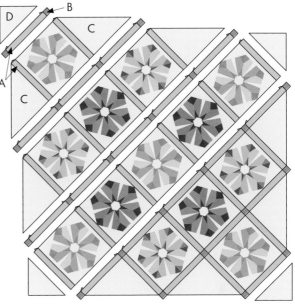

Quilt assembly

Adding the Borders

Refer to "Mitered Borders" on page 93 for detailed instructions as needed.

1. Sew the medium-aqua inner-border strips together end to end and cut four 47"-long strips. Sew the medium-purple middle-border strips together end to end and cut four 52"-long strips.

2. Matching the centers, join a medium-aqua inner-border strip, a medium-purple middle-border strip, and a blue-and-aqua striped outer-border strip as shown to make a border unit. Make four border units.

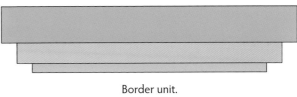

Border unit.
Make 4.

3. Matching the centers, sew the border units to the quilt and miter the corners. Trim the seam allowances to ¼" and press them open.

Quilting and Finishing

Refer to "Basic Quiltmaking Lessons" on page 89 for more information on quilting and finishing your quilt.

1. Mark the Ivy Leaf quilting pattern in the setting triangles and in the middle and outer borders, adding curly vines and lines to connect the motif as shown in the quilting placement diagram.

2. Layer and baste together the backing, batting, and quilt top.

3. Quilt the blocks, sashing, and inner border in the ditch as shown. Quilt the marked motifs.

4. Bind the quilt using the blue-and-aqua striped-batik strips.

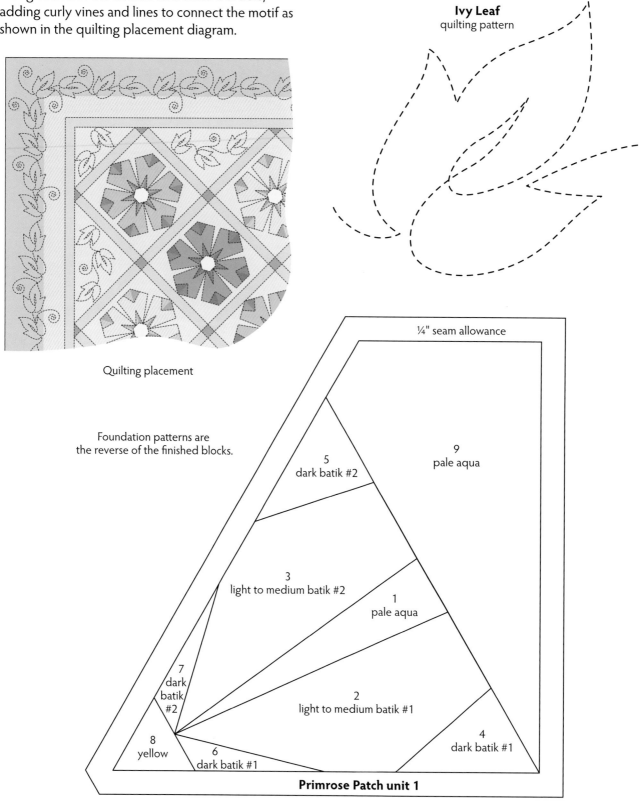

Quilting placement

Ivy Leaf
quilting pattern

Foundation patterns are
the reverse of the finished blocks.

¼" seam allowance

9
pale aqua

5
dark batik #2

3
light to medium batik #2

1
pale aqua

7
dark
batik
#2

2
light to medium batik #1

4
dark batik #1

8
yellow

6
dark batik #1

Primrose Patch unit 1

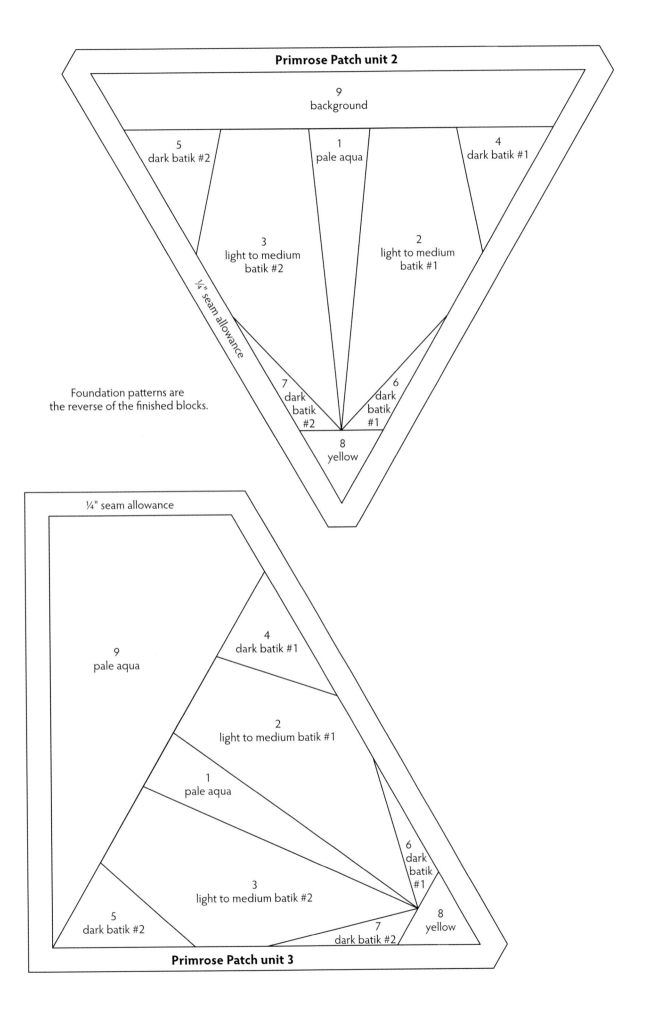

Primrose Patch unit 2

9
background

5
dark batik #2

1
pale aqua

4
dark batik #1

3
light to medium
batik #2

2
light to medium
batik #1

¼" seam allowance

Foundation patterns are
the reverse of the finished blocks.

7
dark
batik
#2

6
dark
batik
#1

8
yellow

¼" seam allowance

9
pale aqua

4
dark batik #1

2
light to medium batik #1

1
pale aqua

6
dark
batik
#1

3
light to medium batik #2

5
dark batik #2

7
dark batik #2

8
yellow

Primrose Patch unit 3

Log Cabin blocks offer such a range of design possibilities. Carolyn has used different pieced blocks in the centers of Log Cabin blocks before, but here she's pieced some of the logs too. Triangles pieced into the logs in this Log Cabin variation form stars and waves—the perfect setting for sailboats.

Designed and sewn by Carolyn Beam, *Quiltmaker* creative editor, and Peg Spradlin; quilted by Peg Spradlin.

Finished Quilt: 58½" x 70½"
Finished Blocks: 12" x 12"

Materials

Yardage is based on 42"-wide fabric.

2 yards of medium-blue batik for outer border and binding

1⅝ yards *total* of assorted medium-blue and dark-blue batiks for blocks

1½ yards *total* of assorted light-blue batiks for blocks

1⅜ yards *total* of assorted aqua and green batiks for background and waves

½ yard *total* of assorted red and orange batiks for boats and waves

½ yard of aqua batik for inner border

⅜ yard *total* of assorted cream batiks for sails

⅜ yard *total* of assorted gold batiks for stars

⅜ yard of gold batik for folded middle border

4 yards of backing fabric

67" x 79" piece of batting

Cutting

Each block uses the same fabrics for the aqua/green background pieces, the star pieces, and each round of light and dark logs.

From the assorted aqua and green batiks, cut *a total of*:

30 squares, 2⅞" x 2⅞" (A)

60 squares, 2½" x 2½" (C)

40 rectangles, 1½" x 4½" (D)

170 squares, 1⅞" x 1⅞" (E)

From the assorted cream batiks, cut *a total of*:

30 squares, 2⅞" x 2⅞" (A)

From the assorted red and orange batiks, cut *a total of*:

20 rectangles, 2½" x 6½" (B)

20 squares, 1⅞" x 1⅞" (E)

From the assorted medium-blue and dark-blue batiks, cut *a total of*:

190 squares, 1⅞" x 1⅞" (E)

80 rectangles, 1½" x 6½" (G)

40 rectangles, 1½" x 7½" (H)

From the assorted gold batiks, cut *a total of*:

100 squares, 1½" x 1½" (F)

Continued on page 72

From the assorted light-blue batiks, cut a total of:
20 rectangles, 1½" x 6½" (G)
20 rectangles, 1½" x 7½" (H)
40 rectangles, 1½" x 8½" (I)
20 rectangles, 1½" x 9½" (J)
20 rectangles, 1½" x 10½" (K)
20 rectangles, 1½" x 2½" (L)

From the aqua batik, cut:
7 inner-border strips, 1½" x 42"

From the gold batik, cut:
7 middle-border strips, 1" x 42"

From the lengthwise grain of the medium-blue batik, cut:
2 outer-border strips, 4½" x 65"
2 outer-border strips, 4½" x 61"
5 binding strips, 2¼" x 56"

Making the Units

Refer to "Triangle Squares" on page 90 to make units 1–3. Notice in the photo on page 71 that in each block the same fabrics are used for the aqua/green background pieces, the star pieces, and each round of light and dark logs.

1. Use the aqua/green A squares and the cream A squares to make 60 of unit 1. Press the seam allowances toward the aqua/green squares.

Unit 1.
Make 60.

2. Use the aqua/green E squares and the medium- and dark-blue E squares to make 340 of unit 2.

Unit 2.
Make 340.

3. Use the red/orange E squares and the medium- and dark-blue E squares to make 40 of unit 3.

Unit 3.
Make 40.

4. Refer to "Stitch and Flip" on page 90 to make units 4–7. Use the red/orange B rectangles and the aqua/green C squares to make 20 of unit 4.

Unit 4.
Make 20.

5. Use the light-blue I rectangles and the gold F squares to make 40 of unit 5.

Unit 5.
Make 40.

6. Use the light-blue L rectangles and the gold F squares to make 20 of unit 6.

Unit 6.
Make 20.

7. Use the light-blue K rectangles and the gold F squares to make 20 of unit 7.

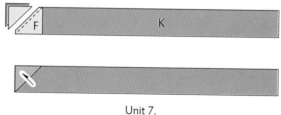

Unit 7.
Make 20.

Making the Blocks

1. Refer to the block assembly diagrams. Join three of unit 1, one of unit 4, one aqua/green C square, and two aqua/green D rectangles to make a sailboat for the block center.

2. Beginning with a light-blue G rectangle and working in a clockwise direction, join the pieces/units to the sailboat center as shown. In this way make 10 of block Y and 10 of block Z, randomly using unit 3 in place of unit 2 in some of the blocks.

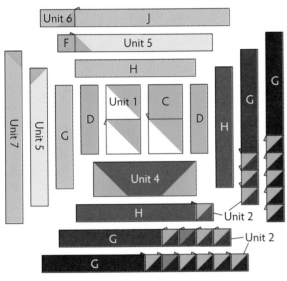

Block Y.
Make 10.

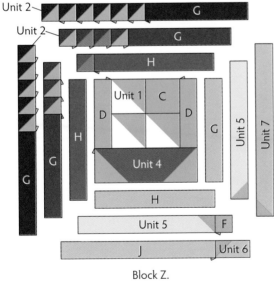

Block Z.
Make 10.

Assembling the Quilt Top

1. Sew four blocks together to make a row. Make three of row 1 and two of row 2. Press the seam allowances in the direction indicated.

Row 1.
Make 3.

Row 2.
Make 2.

2. Join the rows, alternating rows 1 and 2. Press the seam allowances in one direction.

3. Sew the aqua inner-border strips together end to end to make a long strip. Referring to "Squared Borders" on page 93, measure, cut, and sew the aqua inner-border strips to the sides, top, and bottom of the quilt center. Press the seam allowances toward the aqua border.

4. Sew the gold folded-border strips together end to end to make a long strip. Cut two 65"-long strips for the sides and two 53"-long strips for the top and bottom.

5. Fold each strip in half lengthwise, wrong sides together. Matching raw edges, baste the gold folded-border side strips to the quilt top using a ⅛"-wide seam allowance and trimming any extra length. Repeat to add gold folded-border top and bottom strips in the same way.

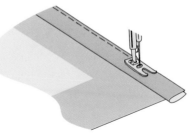

Folded border

6. Measure, cut, and sew the 65"-long medium-blue strips to the sides of the quilt top. Then add the 61"-long medium-blue strips to the top and bottom of the quilt top.

Quilting and Finishing

Refer to "Basic Quiltmaking Lessons" on page 89 for more information on quilting and finishing your quilt.

1. Layer and baste together the backing, batting, and quilt top.

2. Quilt the Rippling Waves quilting pattern on page 75 over the quilt surface as shown in the quilting placement diagram.

3. Bind the quilt using the medium-blue strips.

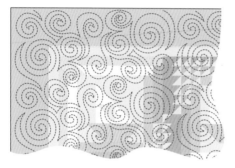

Quilting placement

Design Option

Up, Up, and Away

Replace the sailboat with a rocket ship for a design that's out of this world. Use gold, orange, and red in the triangles for the flames during liftoff. Find the cutting and assembly instructions for one block at quiltmaker.com.

Rippling Waves
quilting pattern

Easy piecing and trimming makes this quilt a breeze to sew. Theresa has taken some of the "fussiness" out of piecing a block that has diagonal seams and angled pieces, without actually cutting or stitching any angles!

Designed by Theresa Eisinger, former *Quiltmaker* graphic designer; made by Kim Waite.

Finished Quilt: 96½" x 96½"
Finished Blocks: 14" x 14"

Materials

Yardage is based on 42"-wide fabric.

3 yards of cream floral for outer border

2¾ yards of green tone-on-tone print for blocks and binding

2⅜ yards of multicolored print for sashing

2¼ yards of teal print for blocks

1¼ yards of coral plaid for blocks

1¼ yards of coral dotted fabric for blocks

1⅛ yards of cream plaid for blocks

1⅛ yards of cream dotted fabric for blocks

⅞ yard of multicolored striped fabric for inner border

9¼ yards of backing fabric

105" x 105" piece of batting

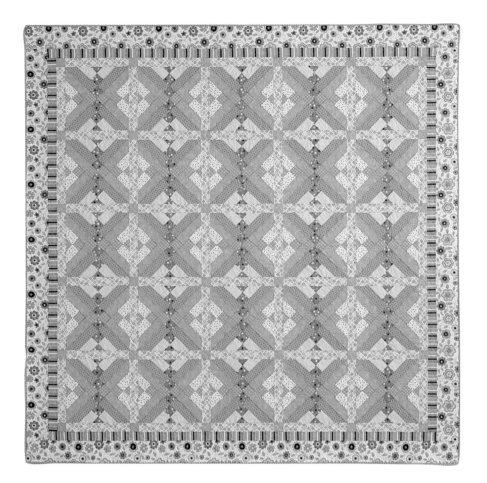

Cutting

From the coral plaid, cut:
  11 strips, 2½" x 42"
  50 squares, 2½" x 2½" (A)

From the coral dotted fabric, cut:
  11 strips, 2½" x 42"
  50 squares, 2½" x 2½" (A)

From the cream plaid, cut:
  7 strips, 2½" x 42"
  50 rectangles, 2½" x 4½" (B)

From the cream dotted fabric, cut:
  7 strips, 2½" x 42"
  50 rectangles, 2½" x 4½" (B)

From the green tone-on-tone print, cut:
  25 strips, 2½" x 42"
  11 binding strips, 2¼" x 42"

From the teal print, cut:
  25 strips, 2½" x 42"
  36 squares, 2½" x 2½" (A)

From the multicolored print, cut:
  60 rectangles, 2½" x 14½" (C)

From the multicolored striped fabric, cut:
  10 inner-border strips, 2½" x 42"

From the *lengthwise grain* of the cream floral, cut:
  2 outer-border strips, 5½" x 89"
  2 outer-border strips, 5½" x 99"

Making the Blocks

1. Join a coral plaid strip and a coral dotted strip along their long edges to make a strip set. Make four of strip set A. Cut the strip sets into 2½"-wide segments to make 50 of unit 1.

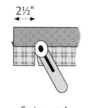

Strip set A.
Make 4.
Cut 50 unit 1 segments.

2. Join a coral dotted strip and a cream plaid strip along their long edges to make a strip set. Make seven of strip set B. Cut the strip sets into 4½"-wide segments to make 50 of unit 2.

Strip set B.
Make 7.
Cut 50 unit 2 segments.

3. Join a coral plaid strip and a cream dotted strip along their long edges to make a strip set. Make seven of strip set C. Cut the strip sets into 4½"-wide segments to make 50 of unit 3.

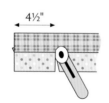

Strip set C.
Make 7.
Cut 50 unit 3 segments.

4. Join a green strip and a teal strip along their long edges to make a strip set. Make 25 of strip set D. Cut the strip sets into 8½"-wide segments to make 100 of unit 4.

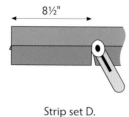

Strip set D.
Make 25.
Cut 100 unit 4 segments.

5. Join the units, coral A squares, and cream B rectangles as shown to make a block. Press the seam allowances in the direction indicated. Trim the block as shown to measure 14½" x 14½". Repeat to make 25 blocks total.

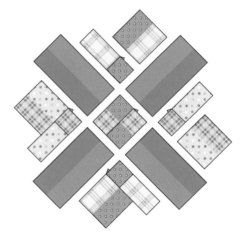

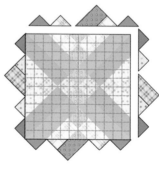

Trim to 14½" x 14½".

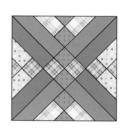

Make 25.

Assembling the Quilt Top

1. Join six teal A squares and five multicolored C rectangles to make a sashing row as shown. Press the seam allowances toward the C rectangles. Make six sashing rows.

Make 6.

2. Join six multicolored C rectangles and five blocks to make a block row. Press the seam allowances toward the C rectangles. Make five block rows.

Make 5.

3. Sew the block rows and sashing rows together, alternating them as shown in the quilt assembly diagram. Press the seam allowances toward the sashing rows.

Quilt assembly

4. Sew the multicolored-striped strips together end to end to make a long strip. Referring to "Squared Borders" on page 93, measure, cut, and sew the strips to the sides, top, and bottom of the quilt top.

5. Measure, cut, and sew the 89"-long cream-floral strips to the sides of the quilt top. Then add the 99"-long cream-floral strips to the top and bottom of the quilt top.

Quilting and Finishing

Refer to "Basic Quiltmaking Lessons" on page 89 for more information on quilting and finishing your quilt.

1. Mark the Linked Hearts quilting pattern on page 80 in the blocks (omitting the red lines), rotating the motif around the block as shown. Mark the sashing and inner border as shown. Mark the Linked Hearts quilting pattern in the outer border, marking the red line instead of the full motif as shown.

2. Layer and baste together the backing, batting, and quilt top.

3. Quilt the marked motifs.

4. Bind the quilt using the green strips.

Quilting placement

¼ Linked Hearts
quilting pattern

Color Option

Change of Pace

Using a darker palette gives this quilt a more masculine appeal.

The staff at *Quiltmaker* joined forces to design this quilt for former editor Lori Scott when she was expecting a baby. Her husband was anxious to see an ultrasound image of the baby, but early on the doctor told them the baby would look pretty much like a kidney bean with arms and legs. From then on, they called their unborn baby "The Bean," and this adorable bean-stalk quilt was made in her honor. To personalize the quilt, you can quilt the baby's name in the narrow borders and appliqué a photo-transfer image of your special new addition.

Designed by the *Quiltmaker* staff; sewn by the *Quiltmaker* staff and Mickie Swall; quilted by Mickie Swall.

Finished Quilt: 45½" x 52½"
Finished Blocks: 6" x 6"

Materials

Yardage is based on 42"-wide fabric.

1½ yards of medium-blue tone-on-tone fabric for sashing, inner border, and outer border

1⅓ yards of light-blue print for middle border

½ yard *total* of assorted green prints for leaf appliqués

½ yard of green print for vine appliqué

20 scraps, at least 6" x 8½", of assorted bright prints for Nine Patch blocks

20 scraps, at least 6" x 6", of assorted light-solid fabrics for Nine Patch blocks

Continued on page 82

Scrap of muslin for photo appliqué (optional)

½ yard of multicolor-striped fabric for binding

3 yards of backing fabric

51" x 58" piece of batting

Cutting

Appliqué patterns C–J are on page 84. For detailed instructions, refer to "Making Plastic Templates" on page 90 as needed.

From *each* of the bright-print scraps, cut:
    5 squares, 2½" x 2½" (A)

From *each* of the light-solid scraps, cut:
    4 squares, 2½" x 2½" (A)

From the *lengthwise grain* of the medium-blue tone-on-tone fabric, cut:
    2 inner-border strips, 1½" x 37"
    2 inner-border strips, 1½" x 32"
    2 outer-border strips, 2½" x 51"
    2 outer-border strips, 2½" x 48"
    4 sashing strips, 1½" x 27½"
    15 rectangles, 1½" x 6½" (B)

From the *lengthwise grain* of the light-blue print, cut:
    1 middle-border strip, 9½" x 39"
    1 middle-border strip, 3½" x 39"
    1 middle-border strip, 9½" x 44"
    1 middle-border strip, 3½" x 44"

From the green print, cut:
    1¾"-wide bias strips to total 88"

From the assorted green prints, cut:
    5 C pieces
    4 C reversed pieces
    7 D pieces
    5 D reversed pieces
    2 E pieces
    3 E reversed pieces
    6 F pieces
    1 F reversed piece
    1 G piece
    2 H pieces
    1 I piece
    1 J piece

From the muslin scrap, cut:
    1 I piece

From the multicolor-striped fabric, cut:
    6 binding strips, 2¼" x 42"

Assembling the Quilt Top

1. Join five matching bright-print A squares and four matching light-solid A squares as shown to make a Nine Patch block. Make 20 blocks total.

Make 20.

2. Sew four blocks and three medium-blue B rectangles together as shown in the quilt assembly diagram to make a row. Press the seam allowances toward the B rectangles. Make five rows.

3. Join the rows and the 27½"-long medium-blue sashing strips to complete the quilt center. Press the seam allowances toward the sashing strips.

4. Referring to "Squared Borders" on page 93, measure, cut, and sew the 1½" x 37" medium-blue inner-border strips to the sides of the quilt top. Then add the 1½" x 32" medium-blue inner-border strips to the top and bottom of the quilt top.

5. Measure, cut, and sew the 9½" x 39" light-blue middle-border strip to the left side and the 3½" x 39" light-blue middle-border strip to the right side of the quilt top. Then add the 9½" x 44" light-blue middle-border strip to the top of the quilt top and the 3½" x 44" light-blue middle-border strip to the bottom of the quilt top.

Personalizing the Quilt

The maker of each block signed her name with a permanent fabric marker.

6. Measure, cut, and sew the 2½" x 51" medium-blue outer-border strips to the sides of the quilt top. Then add the 2½" x 48" medium-blue outer-border strips to the top and bottom of the quilt top.

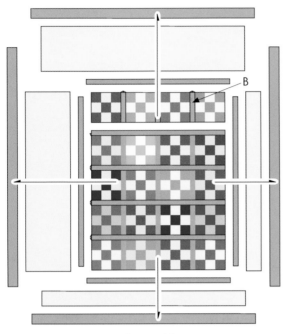

Quilt assembly

Adding the Appliqué

1. Referring to "Bias Strips" on page 93, make the green bias vine.

2. Casually place the vine on the left side and top side of the middle border, using the quilting and appliqué placement diagram and the photo on page 81 as a guide. Stitch the vine in place by hand or machine.

3. Prepare the leaves and beans (C–J) for "Turned-Edge Appliqué" as described on page 92. Casually place the leaves and beans on the quilt top in alphabetical order; hand or machine stitch them in place.

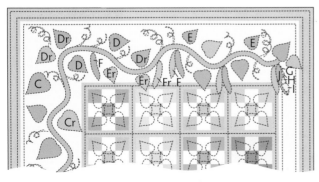

Quilting and appliqué placement

Quilting and Finishing

Refer to "Basic Quiltmaking Lessons" on page 89 for more information on quilting and finishing your quilt.

1. Use the smallest leaf pattern (E) to mark the quilting pattern in the blocks, connecting the leaves with freehand curved lines as shown in the quilting placement diagram.

2. Layer and baste together the backing, batting, and quilt top.

3. Referring to the quilting and appliqué placement diagram, quilt through the middle of the sashing and inner border. Quilt the marked lines in the blocks. In the outer border, quilt three lines 1" apart, starting ¾" from the edge of the quilt top. Quilt around the appliquéd leaves and beans. Quilt free-form vines using green thread. If desired, quilt a name in the middle border.

4. Bind the quilt using the multicolor-striped strips.

Design Option

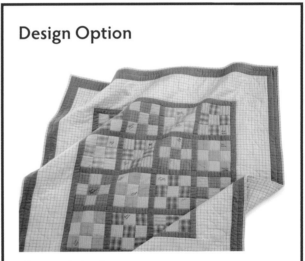

Christian's Quilt

Soft flannels and 6"-wide strips for the middle border create a snuggly variation of this signature quilt as a shower gift for another coworker.

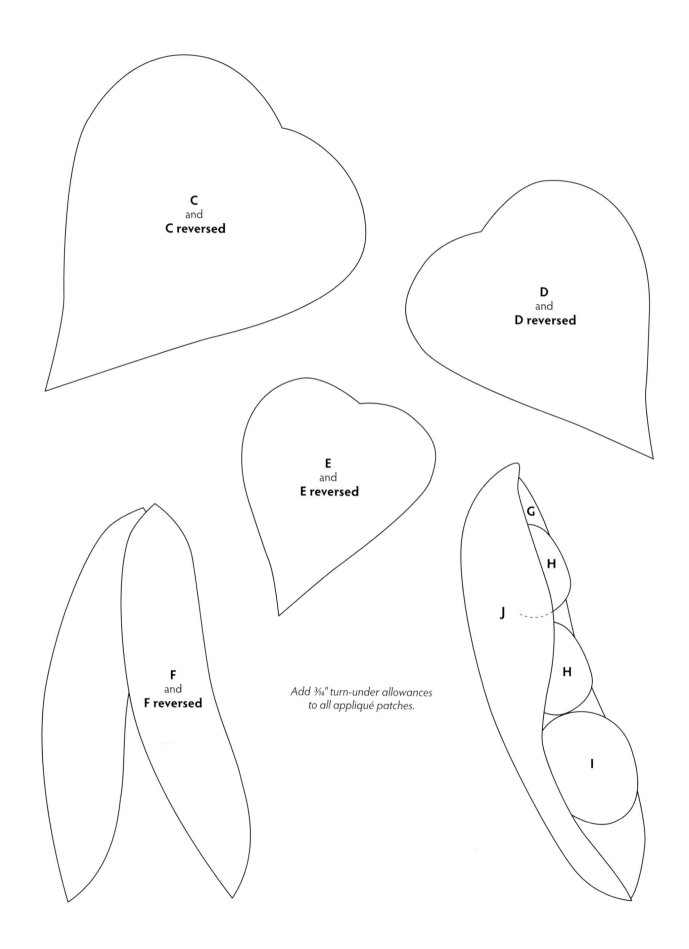

C
and
C reversed

D
and
D reversed

E
and
E reversed

F
and
F reversed

*Add ³⁄₁₆" turn-under allowances
to all appliqué patches.*

G

H

J

H

I

anting a scrappy quilt for the holidays with a showstopping border, Diane designed this wonderful Christmas quilt using her Electric Quilt software while watching television on a snowy winter night. Dig into your fabric stash to make this scrappy delight. Notice that the dark-green squares run diagonally in one direction across the quilt, while the red squares run diagonally in the other direction.

Designed by Diane Harris, *Quiltmaker* interactive editor; sewn by Diane Harris and Kim Waite; quilted by Kim Waite.

Finished Quilt: 63½" x 72½"
Finished Blocks: 9" x 9"

Materials

Yardage is based on 42"-wide fabric.

2 yards of multicolored print for middle border

1½ yards *total* of assorted cream prints for blocks

1⅜ yards *total* of assorted light-green prints for blocks

1¼ yards of green tone-on-tone print for outer border and binding

⅝ yard *total* of assorted dark-green prints for blocks

⅝ yard *total* of assorted red prints for blocks

⅝ yard of red tone-on-tone print for inner border

4¾ yards of backing fabric

72" x 81" piece of batting

Cutting

From the assorted light-green prints, cut *a total of:*
  240 rectangles, 2" x 3½" (A)

From the assorted cream prints, cut *a total of:*
  480 squares, 2" x 2" (B)

From the assorted dark-green prints, cut *a total of:*
  180 squares, 2" x 2" (B)

From the assorted red prints, cut *a total of:*
  180 squares, 2" x 2" (B)

From the red tone-on-tone print, cut:
  6 inner-border strips, 2½" x 42"

From the *lengthwise grain* **of the multicolored print, cut:**
  2 middle-border strips, 5½" x 61"
  2 middle-border strips, 5½" x 62"

From the green tone-on-tone print, cut:
  8 outer-border strips, 2½" x 42"
  8 binding strips, 2¼" x 42"

Making the Quilt Center

1. Referring to "Stitch and Flip" on page 90, join a light-green A rectangle and a cream B square to make unit 1. Press the seam allowances toward the resulting cream triangle. See "Just One Thread" on page 87 for helpful information on piecing the unit accurately. Make 120 of unit 1. Repeat the process to make 120 of unit 2. (Notice that unit 2 is a mirror image of unit 1.)

Unit 1.
Make 120.

Unit 2.
Make 120.

2. Join each unit 1 to a unit 2 as shown to make 120 units. Press the seam allowances to one side.

Make 120.

3. Referring to the diagrams, make the appropriate number of each four-patch unit. Press the seam allowances in the directions indicated.

Four-patch 1. Make 60.   Four-patch 2. Make 60.   Four-patch 3. Make 30.

4. Join the various four-patch units and the units from step 2 in rows, making sure to orient the pieces as shown. Press the seam allowances toward the four-patch units. Join the rows to complete the block; press. Make 30 blocks total.

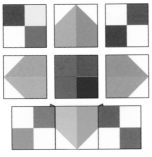

Make 30.

5. Join five blocks as shown to make a row; press. Make six rows. Sew the rows together; press.

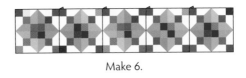

Make 6.

Adding the Borders

1. Join the red inner-border strips end to end to make a long strip. Referring to "Squared Borders" on page 93, measure, cut, and sew the strips to the sides, top, and bottom of the quilt center.

2. Measure, cut, and sew the 61"-long multicolored middle-border strips to the sides of the quilt top. Then add the 62"-long multicolored middle-border strips to the top and bottom of the quilt top.

3. Join the green outer-border strips end to end to make a long strip. Measure, cut, and sew the strips to the sides, top, and bottom of the quilt top.

Quilting and Finishing

Refer to "Basic Quiltmaking Lessons" on page 89 for more information on quilting and finishing your quilt.

1. Mark the Garden Swirl quilting pattern on page 88 in each block and over the borders, matching centers and rotating to complete the motif as shown in the quilting placement diagram.

2. Layer and baste together the backing, batting, and quilt top.

3. Quilt the marked motifs.

4. Bind the quilt using the green strips.

Quilting placement

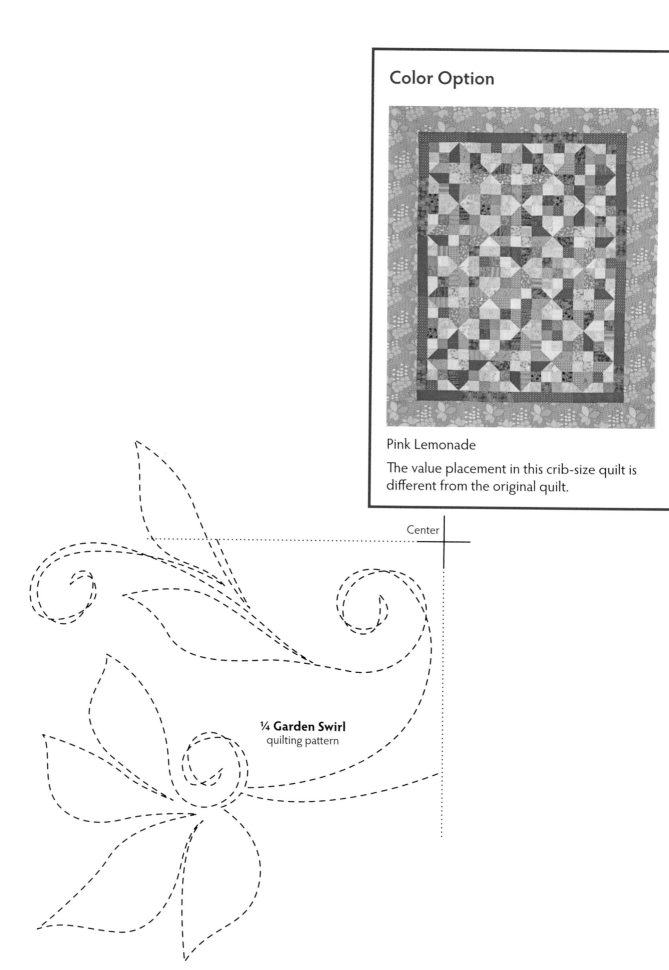

Color Option

Pink Lemonade

The value placement in this crib-size quilt is different from the original quilt.

Center

¼ **Garden Swirl**
quilting pattern

W**e recommend that you read all of the instructions before starting a project, and that you cut and sew one block before cutting all of your fabric.**

Use a rotary cutter, mat, and an acrylic ruler to cut the shape to the size indicated in the cutting list. The patterns list finished block sizes, which are typically ½" smaller than unfinished block sizes because they do not include seam allowances.

Basic Quilting Supplies

- Rotary cutter and mat
- Acrylic ruler: Many shapes and sizes are available; a good one to start with is 6" x 24" with ¼" and ⅛" markings.
- Scissors: separate pairs for paper and fabric
- Sewing machine
- ¼" presser foot
- Walking foot
- Darning foot
- Pins
- Ironing board and iron
- Marking tools (pencils, markers, etc.)
- Needles
- Thimble
- Safety pins
- Template plastic
- Thread

Preparing Your Fabric

We recommend that you prewash your fabrics. A shrinkage factor is included in our yardage computations.

Cutting

Measure, mark, and cut the binding and border strips before cutting pieces from the same fabric. Cut larger pieces before cutting smaller ones. For best use of the fabric, arrange pieces with cutting lines close or touching.

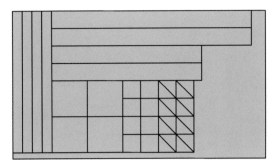

One or more straight sides of the piece should follow the lengthwise (parallel to the selvages) or crosswise (perpendicular to the selvages) grain of the fabric, especially the sides that will be on the outside edges of the quilt block. We indicate lengthwise or crosswise grain with an arrow on the pattern piece, if appropriate.

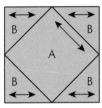

To find the grain line of your fabric for rotary cutting, hold the fabric with selvages parallel in front of you. Keeping the selvages together, slide the edge closest to you to one side or the other until the fabric hangs straight, without wrinkles or folds. Then lay the fabric down on your cutting mat and cut perpendicular to the fold line. Use this cut edge as your straight-of-grain line.

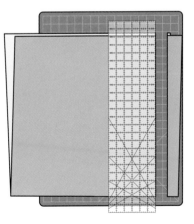

Many pieces can be cut from strips of fabric by rotary cutting. First, cut a strip of fabric the width needed. Then, crosscut the strip into pieces the required size.

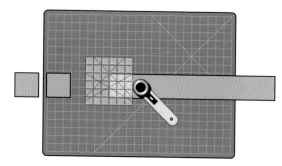

To cut from a template, place the template face down on the wrong side of the fabric and trace with a sharp pencil. Reverse templates should be placed face up on the wrong side of the fabric before tracing.

Making Plastic Templates

To make templates for machine piecing or appliqué, trace the patterns provided onto template plastic with a fine-tipped, permanent-ink pen, making sure to trace the lines exactly. Mark the fabric grain line as shown on the pattern. Use utility scissors to cut out the templates, cutting exactly on the drawn lines. When placing the templates on the fabrics, pay careful attention to the grain lines noted on each template, if appropriate.

Machine Piecing

If the presser foot is ¼" wide, align the cut edges of fabric with the edge of the presser foot. If the presser foot is not the correct size, place masking tape on the throat plate of your machine ¼" from the needle to use as a guide.

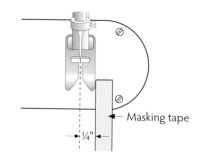

← Masking tape

¼"

TRIANGLE SQUARES

A triangle square is made up of two half-square triangles sewn together. Here is a method of making triangle squares that is fast and accurate.

1. Cut the squares the size specified in the cutting instructions.

2. Layer two same-sized squares right sides together with the lighter square on top and the raw edges aligned. On the wrong side of the lighter square, draw a diagonal line from corner to corner.

3. Sew ¼" from each side of the drawn diagonal line. Cut the squares apart on the marked line.

4. Press the seam allowances toward the darker fabric, unless instructed otherwise. Each pair of squares will yield two triangle-square units.

STITCH AND FLIP

The stitch-and-flip technique is a common way to achieve a triangle-shaped corner by layering a square on top of a rectangle.

1. Draw a diagonal line from corner to corner on the wrong side of the square.

2. Place the marked square on one end of a rectangle, right sides together and raw edges aligned.

3. Sew on the marked line and trim away the corner fabric, leaving a ¼" seam allowance. Press the resulting triangle open.

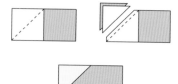

Pressing

Press all seam allowances to one side, usually toward the darker fabric, unless otherwise instructed. When joining blocks and/or rows, seam allowances are pressed to allow seams to nest, which reduces bulk in the quilt top.

Foundation-Piecing Basics

This method makes some difficult blocks easy to piece. No templates or rotary-cut pieces are required to sew accurate points and intricate designs. With a little practice and by following a few guidelines, you can create stunning quilts that look like only an expert could have pieced them.

MAKING COPIES

First make copies of the foundation pattern; you'll need one foundation for each block or unit you intend to sew.

Materials appropriate for paper foundations include tracing, copy-machine, onionskin, vellum, tissue, and parchment paper. Also available are laser-printer papers made specifically for reproducing foundations for this technique. Check quilt shops and office-supply stores for these options.

Many methods are available to reproduce foundations. Some methods are more accurate than others, and some are more expensive; experiment to decide which one is right for your needs.

- Trace the foundation pattern directly onto tracing or other transparent paper and repeat to make the needed number of foundations.

- Use a photocopy machine to duplicate the foundation pattern. Always test for accuracy by first making one copy, and then comparing it with the original over a light source. If the copy differs more than 1/16", use another photocopier.

- Using a computer, scan the foundation pattern, and then print copies from a computer printer. As with the photocopier, check for accuracy.

GETTING SET UP

Take a moment to prepare your machine and work space for the best results.

Set your machine stitch length to 18 to 20 stitches to the inch (1.5 mm) for stitching through paper

foundations. This perforates the paper and makes it easy to remove.

Choose a needle that's appropriate for the fabric you're sewing. See "Use the Right Needle" below for guidance.

If you have one, use an open-toe presser foot for the best visibility.

Choose a thread that blends with most of the fabrics; light tan or gray is ideal for almost all piecing.

Place an ironing board and iron within reach so you can easily press after sewing each piece. Or, you can use a pressing tool or your fingernail.

Finally, have a lamp or a sunny window nearby so you can see the piece size and placement of pieces through the paper foundation.

Use the Right Needle

For foundation piecing choose a needle that's appropriate for the fabric you're sewing, such as a size 70/10 or 80/12 Sharp for cotton fabrics. A larger needle can make it hard to stitch accurately, especially when stitching small sections and short lines. It's the stitch length that's important for tearing away the paper after stitching, not the size of the holes you're creating. (Think of a spiral-bound notebook: big holes, ragged edges. A micro-perforated edge with tiny holes will tear cleanly.)

FABRIC PREPARATION

Many quiltmakers like to cut fabric pieces before starting to sew, while others like the cut-as-you-go method—either way is fine. These suggestions will help you guesstimate the piece size and avoid wasted fabric.

For each foundation piece, add about 1/2" to each side when cutting out the approximate shape. Some shapes that are sewn at odd angles may require even more fabric. For those pieces that lie along the edge of the foundation, be sure that the fabric extends beyond the outer line, plus a little extra for trimming after the foundation is completed.

FOUNDATION PIECING

1. Place fabric piece 1 right side up on the unprinted side of the foundation. Hold the foundation and fabric piece up to the light to see if the fabric covers area 1 on the foundation, plus at least ¼" seam allowance on all sides. From the paper side, pin fabric piece 1 in place through the center.

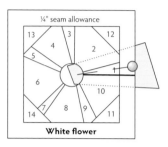

2. Turn the foundation over, fabric side up; using a piece of fabric sufficient to cover area 2 and its seam allowances, position piece 2 right sides together on piece 1. Both fabrics should extend at least ¼" beyond the seam line between areas 1 and 2. Holding the layers along this seam line, flip fabric piece 2 over to see if it's large enough to cover area 2, plus extra for the seam allowance. If not, either readjust the fabric placement or cut another piece and check again.

3. Holding the layers in place, turn the foundation over so the paper side is facing up. Carefully slide the layers under the presser foot and lower the foot; begin sewing at least ¼" before the start of the printed seam line. Sew on the line and ¼" beyond the end of the line.

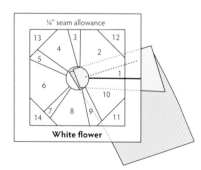

4. Remove the foundation from the machine and clip the threads. Fold the paper back on the just-sewn line and trim the extra fabric ¼" from the fold. You can use scissors to cut the seam allowances by eye or use rotary-cutting tools for trimming.

5. Turn the foundation over, open the just-sewn piece to be right side out, and press the layers flat. If you're using an iron, use a dry one. Steam may warp or distort the foundation.

6. Repeat these steps to add piece 3 and the remaining pieces in numerical order until you've completed the foundation. Do not stitch along the outer seam line. Use a rotary cutter and ruler to trim the excess fabric and paper ¼" from the outer seam line of the foundation, creating a seam allowance.

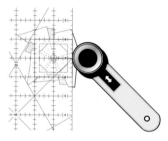

Turned-Edge Appliqué

It's helpful to have as many bias edges as possible on the perimeter of your appliqué pieces. Make a plastic template of each pattern as described in "Making Plastic Templates" on page 90. Place the template face up on the right side of the fabric (face down on the right side for a reverse piece) and lightly draw around the template. Turn-under seam allowances are not included on appliqué patterns. Cut out each piece, adding a ³⁄₁₆" seam allowance outside the marked line.

On inside curves, clip the seam allowances almost to the marked seam line. Turn under the seam allowance and finger-press.

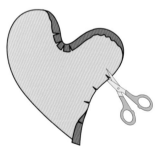

Pin or baste appliqué pieces onto the background fabric. To appliqué by hand, use a blind stitch and a thread color that matches the appliqué piece. To appliqué by machine, use a small zigzag or blind hemstitch and a matching or invisible thread.

Blind stitch

If the background fabric shows through the appliquéd piece, carefully cut away the background fabric to within ³⁄₁₆" of the appliqué piece, or use two layers of appliqué fabric.

BIAS STRIPS

Bias strips are cut at a 45° angle to the straight of grain of the fabric. They're stretchy and therefore ideal for binding curved edges or creating curved appliqué stems.

Make your first cut by aligning a 45° guideline on your acrylic ruler with the cut edge or selvage of your fabric. Use this new bias edge to cut strips the required width.

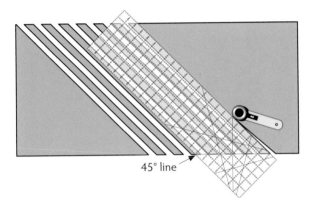

45° line

Prepare bias strips for appliqué by folding them in half lengthwise, wrong sides together. Stitch ¼" from the raw edges. Position the seam allowances as shown and press them toward the center. Trim the seam allowances to ⅛".

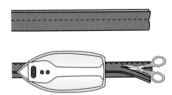

Squared Borders

Squared borders are added first to the sides of the quilt center, and then to the top and bottom. Some of the border strips are cut along the crosswise grain and joined where extra length is needed. Others are cut lengthwise and do not need to be pieced. All of the border measurements in the cutting lists include a few extra inches so that the

borders can be cut to fit the center measurement of the quilt.

Lay the quilt top flat on a large table or the floor. Lay both side border strips down the vertical center of the quilt top and smooth carefully into place. Slip a small cutting mat under the quilt top (you'll need to do this at the top and the bottom edges) and use a rotary cutter and ruler to trim the border strips to the same length as the quilt top. Matching centers and ends, sew the border strips to the sides of the quilt top. Gently press the seam allowances away from the quilt center.

Repeat this process along the horizontal center of the quilt top, including the just-added borders. Repeat for any remaining borders.

Mitered Borders

Mitered borders are added by sewing border strips to all sides of the quilt center, and then mitering each corner. When joining each border strip to the quilt, begin and end stitching ¼" from the quilt-top corners, and backstitch. Referring to the diagrams, fold the quilt right sides together diagonally at one corner. Flip the seam allowances toward the quilt top, match seam lines, and pin through both layers about 3" from the corner. Place a ruler along the folded edge of the quilt top, intersecting the final stitch in the border seam line and extending across the border strip.

Draw a line from the seam line to the outer edge of the border as shown. Pin the layers together along the marked line. Starting at the inside edge with a backstitch, sew along the line to the outer edge of the border. Trim the seam allowances to ¼" and press them open. Repeat for all corners.

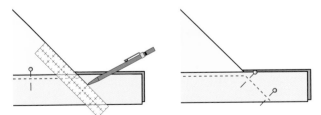

Marking Quilting Designs

Trace the quilting motif onto tracing paper. Place the tracing paper under the quilt top with a light source behind. Lightly mark the design on the quilt top with a hard-lead pencil or a marker of your choice. Test any marking product for removability before using it on your quilt.

Straight lines may be marked as you quilt by using masking tape, and then removing it after quilting along its edge.

Backing and Basting

Make the quilt backing 4" to 8" larger than the quilt top. Remove the selvages to avoid puckers. Usually two or three lengths must be sewn together. Press the seam allowances open. Place the backing wrong side up on a flat surface, stretch slightly, and tape or pin it in place. Smooth the batting over the backing. Center the quilt top right side up on top of the batting. Pin the layers as necessary to secure them while basting.

BASTING FOR MACHINE QUILTING
Machine-quilted tops can be basted with rustproof safety pins. Begin at the center and place pins 3" to 4" apart, avoiding lines to be quilted.

BASTING FOR HAND QUILTING
Beginning in the center of the quilt, baste horizontal and vertical lines 4" to 6" apart.

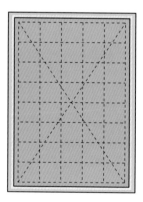

Quilting

Quilting in the ditch refers to quilting right next to the seam line on the side without seam allowances. Outline quilting refers to quilting ¼" from the seam line.

MACHINE QUILTING
Before machine quilting, bring the bobbin thread to the top of the quilt so it doesn't get caught as you quilt. To do this, lower the presser foot, hold the top thread, and take one stitch down and up; lift the presser foot to release the thread tension and tug on the top thread to draw a loop of the bobbin thread to the top of the quilt. Pull the bobbin thread to the top. Lower the needle into the same hole created by the initial stitch, lower your presser foot, and start quilting. A walking foot is used for straight-line or ditch quilting. Start and end your quilting lines with ¼" of very short stitches to secure.

HAND QUILTING
Hand quilting is accomplished using a short running stitch with a single strand of thread that goes through all three layers.

Use a short needle (8 or 9 Between) with about 18" of thread. Make a small knot in the thread and take a long first stitch (about 1") through the quilt top and batting only, coming up where the quilting will begin. Tug on the thread to pull the knotted end between the layers. Take short, even stitches that are the same size on the top and back of the quilt. Push the needle with a thimble on your middle finger; guide the fabric in front of the needle with the thumb of one hand above the quilt and with the middle finger of your other hand under the quilt.

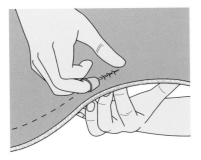

To end a line of quilting, make a small knot in the thread close to the quilt top, push the needle through the top and batting only, and bring it to the surface about 1" away. Tug the thread until the knot pulls through the quilt top, burying the knot in the batting. Clip the thread close to the surface of the quilt top.

Binding

Baste around the quilt about ³⁄₁₆" from the outer edges. Trim the batting and backing ¼" beyond the edge of the quilt top.

1. To prepare the binding strips, place the ends of two binding strips perpendicular to each other, right sides together. Stitch diagonally as shown and trim the seam allowances to ¼". In this way, join all the strips and press the seam allowances open.

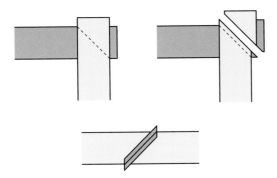

2. Cut the beginning of the binding strip at a 45° angle. Fold the binding strip in half lengthwise, wrong sides together, and press.

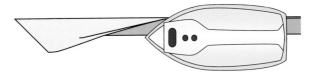

3. Starting in the middle of a side and leaving a 6" tail of binding loose, align the raw edges of the binding with the edge of the quilt top. Begin sewing the binding to the quilt using a ¼" seam allowance. Stop ¼" from the first corner and backstitch. Remove the needle from the quilt and cut the threads.

4. Fold the binding up, and then back down, even with edge of the quilt. Begin stitching ¼" from the binding fold, backstitch to secure, and continue sewing. Repeat at all corners.

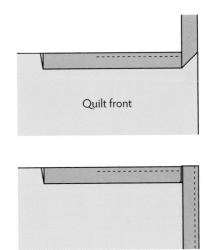

Quilt front

5. When nearing the starting point, leave at least 12" of the quilt edge unbound and a 10" to 12" binding tail. Smooth the beginning tail over the ending tail. Following the cut edge of the beginning tail, draw a line on the ending tail at a 45° angle. To add seam allowance, draw a cutting line ½" from the first line; make sure it guides you to cut the binding tail ½" *longer* than the first line. Cut on this second line.

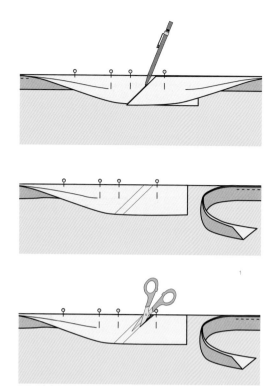

6. To join the ends, place them right sides together. Join the strips, offsetting them ¼" as shown. Press the seam allowances open. Press this section of binding in half, and then finish sewing it to the quilt. Trim away excess backing and batting *in the corners only* to eliminate bulk.

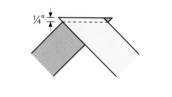

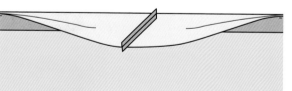

7. Fold the binding to the back of the quilt, enclosing the extra batting and backing. Blindstitch the fold of the binding to the back of the quilt, covering the line of machine stitching.

Quilt back

Hanging Sleeve

Sleeve edges can be caught in the seam when you sew the binding to the quilt. Cut and join enough 9"-wide strips of fabric to equal the width of the quilt. Hem the short ends of the sleeve by folding under ½", pressing, and then folding and pressing once more; topstitch close to the edge of the hem. Fold the sleeve in half lengthwise, wrong sides together, matching raw edges. Center the sleeve on the back and top of the quilt and baste. Sew the binding to the quilt. Once the binding has been sewn, smooth the sleeve against the backing and blindstitch along the bottom and the ends of the sleeve, catching some of the batting in the stitches.